How To Prepare Your UK Self Assessment Tax Return

By H.M. Reynolds

INDEX:

1

About the author:

H.M. Reynolds is a qualified accountant with over fifteen years financial and accounting experience.

Introduction:

Modern tax law requires a shelf of thick textbooks full of tiny writing. It may surprise you to know that there is so much tax law that even the experts can't know it all. When taking their exams Chartered Tax Advisers have to know where to find the rules rather than being required to memorise them all. So unfortunately, I cannot give you a comprehensive guide to all aspects of tax here.
Because of this complexity, even preparing a simple tax return can be full of pitfalls and potential missed opportunities. Here I hope to give you a glimpse of what would be available to you if you were to hire a qualified accountant and perhaps to enable you to evade some common mistakes.

This is a guide to assist a UK resident in preparing their UK self-assessment tax return, which has been updated to reflect the tax rules applying in the 5 April 2023 tax year.
It is designed to assist those with fairly simple tax affairs. If you have a more complicated business, you may wish to consult a qualified accountant. Details of some of the professional bodies are given in the appendices.

Naturally, I cannot bear any responsibility for any losses or costs that you might bear in attempting to follow this book; sorry to burden you with a disclaimer so soon, but it seems an unfortunate necessity of our modern culture. I would advise you to double check any points of tax law that I cover before relying on them, particularly as your specific circumstances may be different to those I am describing in this book, and also because of the ever-changing nature of law.
However, now that I have got that out of the way, we can continue.

This book will begin with an assessment of the types of information you need to gather before completing your tax return and continue by following the format of the tax return, explaining each section where necessary. I will only comment on the fields which require explanation or where there is an interesting tangent which will hopefully provide you with useful information on an aspect of tax.

I shall omit details of some of the more complicated sections. For example, as I mentioned above, I am assuming that the user of this book is a UK resident and therefore you will not have to complete the non-residents pages.

My purpose is to show from an accountant's point of view what the significance of each section is, and any points that my experience brings to mind.
Some explanations may be duplicated where an entry is relevant in more than one of the optional sections. This is to make sure the information is shown where it applies. I apologise if this means you have to read anything twice, for example if you are self-employed and own a rental property.

If you feel you still need help, a qualified accountant will be your best bet. It is usual practice to grant a free initial interview at which you can talk about your tax affairs and what they can do for you.
You can also try contacting HMRC; however there can often be long waits on the phone to reach one of their staff. Once you eventually get through, they will be able to advise on procedural aspects of filing your tax return. Note that there have been court cases which call into question whether or not you can rely on tax advice given by HMRC, and they often reserve the right to change their mind!
However, as you probably bought this book to avoid the cost of an accountant, I will leave any further advice on that matter aside.

Finally, I will be including example pages from this year's tax return within this book, but you may wish to have a paper or electronic copy to hand to refer to. The nature of my chosen publication medium means that the example pages may not always be as easy to read as a physical copy.
You can use this book whether you are completing your tax return on paper or online. The treatment of the various income and expenses items will be the same, although the layout on the screen may be different.

Do I need to file a tax return?

Firstly and obviously, there is no point filing a tax return if you don't need to!

Why you might have to:
If HMRC has sent you a request to file a tax return you will need to do so.

If you have income not covered by tax deducted at source you should also complete a tax return. PAYE deductions from an employed person's salary are an example of a tax deduction at source.

If you think there will be a tax benefit to you in filing a return, you may wish to do so: for example, if you have more than one job and may have paid too much tax because of the tax codes applied to your wages.

You will not have to file a return if all your income is covered by PAYE or otherwise deducted at source. If in this circumstance you have been issued with a request to file one, you should get in contact with HMRC and ask if they will cancel the request.

Since 6 April 2016 there has been a personal savings allowance for bank and building interest, which is £1,000 for basic rate taxpayers and £500 for higher rate taxpayers.
In addition, there is a £2,000 tax free allowance for dividends received. (This will be reduced to £1,000 for the 05 April 2024 year and down to £500 for the 05 April 2025 year).
Roughly speaking if your interest and dividends are within those thresholds and your only other income has tax deducted at source, then you won't need to file a return.
The main exception to this would be if your total income including the interest and dividends took you into the higher or additional rate tax band.

There is also a £1,000 trading allowance for businesses such as Ebay traders. If your gross income from this sort of business is £1,000 or less you do not have to report it. There is a similar allowance of £1,000 for small amounts of property income, and if you rent a room in the property you live in, you can earn £7,500 rent without having to pay tax or fill in a tax return.

Information required before you start:

Let's look at each section, so we can produce a checklist of what might be required. It might not be everything you need for your specific circumstances, but these would be the common items required by an accountant.

Personal information:

To begin with you will need to have these to hand:
- Your UTR (Unique Taxpayer Registration number). This would be on any correspondence from HMRC requesting that you file a tax return or on the letter you received when you first registered for self-assessment.
- Your National Insurance number.
- If you expect to get a refund on tax for some reason and wish to receive the funds by bank transfer, you may also wish to have your bank account details to hand.

General:

- Tax certificates showing any bank interest received. Note that from 6 April 2016 onwards you will only pay tax on this if you receive more than £1,000 in interest. You do not need to report interest received from an ISA as these are tax free.
- Failing tax certificates being available, you can get bank statements covering the period and add up the interest received in the tax year. Bank statements may be useful for other purposes, as noted below, but for recording bank interest received, they should cover the tax year from 6 April to 5 April.
- Tax certificates for any dividends received (where payment dates fall into the year ended 5th April). You will only pay tax on dividends if the amount received exceeds the dividends allowance, which for the 5 April 2023 tax year is £2,000 (it reduces to £1,000 from 6 April 23, and then to £500 a year later).
- Details of any state or other pensions receivable in the tax year. Again, if you do not have any tax deducted at source from your pensions, you will be able to extract the information from your bank statements.

Rental Property Income:

- Letting agents' statements for each month in the tax year.
- Bank statements for any accounts in which you have received rental income.
- Cheque books and paying in books for those bank accounts.
- Invoices for any expenses relating to the properties.
- Mortgage statements for the properties, if possible showing the interest charged in the tax year. You might only get mortgage statements once a year, in which case you may have to estimate part of the interest in the tax year. Even if the mortgage statements do not run to the tax year, some mortgage providers will be able to produce tax certificates that do.

Self-Employed Income:

- Bank statements for bank accounts which you have used to receive self-employed income and from which you have paid self-employed expenses.
- Cheque books and paying in books for those bank accounts.
- Credit card statements for any credit cards used in your business.
- Bank loan statements for any loans you have taken out to support your business.
- Sales invoices for the year.
- Purchase invoices for the year.
- Any cashbooks detailing your bank and cash expenses.
- VAT returns & workings*

* - for this guide I am assuming that you have a fairly simple business and that you are below the VAT threshold, but you might have decided to register voluntarily, for example if the nature of your business is such that you are likely to receive regular VAT refunds.

Partnership Income:

This is where you are self-employed in conjunction with one or more other individuals.

What you will need here is much the same as for general self-employed people.

When you registered the partnership for self-assessment, your partnership would have been given a Unique Tax Payer Reference (UTR) of its own. This is a separate UTR to your personal one, so you will need both to hand.

Foreign Income:

If you have foreign bank accounts or shares in foreign businesses, you will probably already have collected this information for the general category I summarised above, but just to note that this goes in a separate part of the tax return, so you might want to separate them out.

Foreign dividends, interest and rental property income are not treated in a vastly different way to UK income from such sources, but they are entered on the foreign pages of the tax return rather than on the main return. Because I am trying to keep things simple, I will not be going into this in a lot of detail. As with any of the sections of the tax return, you will find notes on how to complete it on the HMRC website.

If your total income from UK and foreign property was £1,000 or less, this may be exempted by the Property Income Allowance, and will not therefore need to be reported on a tax return.

If your only foreign income was untaxed foreign interest of up to £2,000 you can enter this in box 3 on page TR03 of the main tax return and there will be no need for you to complete the foreign income pages. Likewise, if your only foreign income is dividends up to £2,000, you can enter this in box 5 of page TR03 and there will be no need for you to complete the foreign income pages.

Capital gains:

If you sold any assets or property in the year, you will need details of:
- The original cost.
- Any purchase expenses – e.g. legal fees.
- The sale price.
- Any sale expenses.
- Any amounts spent to conduct improvements – e.g. adding an extension to a house.

Cars are exempt from capital gains tax and if you have only owned one house at a time then it will be exempted by virtue of Private Residence Relief (Which used to be called Principal Private Residence relief). This is one of many areas which can have complicated tax results, so I will restrict myself to the simplest situations, such as when you live in one house and have a rental property that you have never lived in.
One example of a complication that I am talking about would be if you had owned a series of different rental properties and moved around living in different ones in different years – in that case Private Residence Relief would not be so straight forward to calculate.

When Private Residence Relief is calculated, the last few months of property ownership automatically qualify, which is designed to cater to the common situation where, when you are in a property chain, you may briefly own two houses before the new owners take over your old house.
Since 6 April 2020, this final period exemption is 9 months.

Since 27 October 2021, capital gains on disposal of property must be reported within 60 days of the property being sold. Any capital gains tax due also need to be paid within this period. When completing your annual tax return, you can then correct any estimates used in the capital gains tax reports made during the year, for example if the costs were higher than you recorded when you originally reported the sale.

9

Main Tax Return – form SA 100:

Page TR 01:

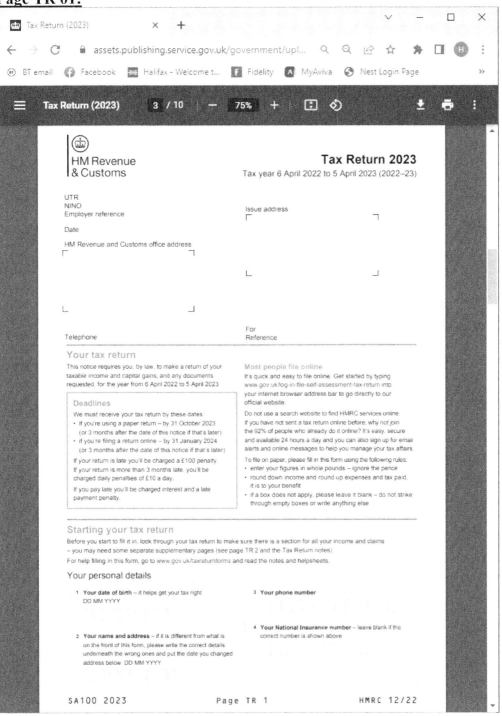

This first page contains the crucial information that HMRC needs to identify you as an individual taxpayer.

At the top left you will see the requirement to include your UTR (Unique Taxpayer Reference), National Insurance Number and Employer reference.

This section also includes the address of the HMRC office which will deal with your return and your own address. If you have been sent a request to complete a tax return by HMRC, some or all of this information will be filled in already. In which case, you just need to make sure it is correct.

The UTR will have been sent to you when you registered for income tax. If HMRC has sent you a letter notifying that you need to file a return, it should be on that letter as well, even if they have not posted you a paper copy of a tax return.

The employer reference relates to your PAYE scheme if you are an employer. If you are not, then you can leave this blank.
(Apologies if some of the points I make are obvious to you, there will be people for whom nothing on the tax return form appears straightforward).

Note the deadlines box on this page. If you are filing a paper return for some reason, you only have until 31 October to get it to HMRC – 3 months less than a return filed online. You will also have to allow time for the return to travel through the post.
Of course, the advantage of an electronic return is that you can submit it and receive an email confirmation of receipt the same day. It will be good practice for you to keep a copy of that confirmation, in case you later receive a late tax return filing penalty in error.

Page TR02:

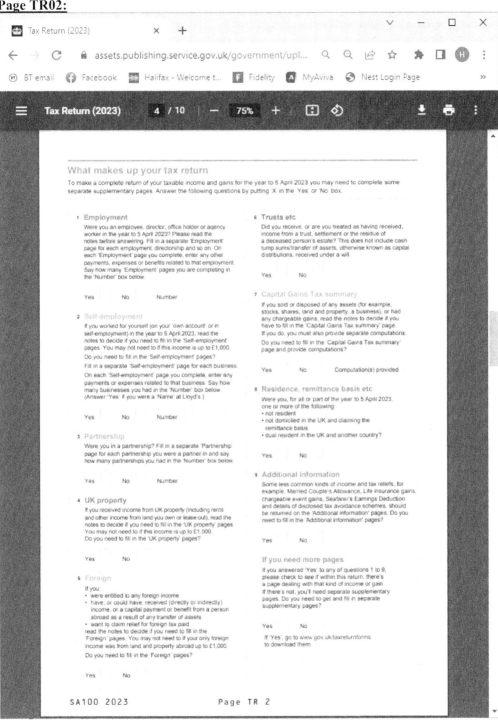

What makes up your tax return

To make a complete return of your taxable income and gains for the year to 5 April 2023 you may need to complete some separate supplementary pages. Answer the following questions by putting 'X' in the 'Yes' or 'No' box.

1 Employment

Were you an employee, director, office holder or agency worker in the year to 5 April 2023? Please read the notes before answering. Fill in a separate 'Employment' page for each employment, directorship and so on. On each 'Employment' page you complete, enter any other payments, expenses or benefits related to that employment. Say how many 'Employment' pages you are completing in the 'Number' box below.

Yes   No   Number

2 Self-employment

If you worked for yourself (on your 'own account' or in self-employment) in the year to 5 April 2023, read the notes to decide if you need to fill in the 'Self-employment' pages. You may not need to if this income is up to £1,000.
Do you need to fill in the 'Self-employment' pages?
Fill in a separate 'Self-employment' page for each business. On each 'Self-employment' page you complete, enter any payments or expenses related to that business. Say how many businesses you had in the 'Number' box below. (Answer 'Yes' if you were a 'Name' at Lloyd's.)

Yes   No   Number

3 Partnership

Were you in a partnership? Fill in a separate 'Partnership' page for each partnership you were a partner in and say how many partnerships you had in the 'Number' box below.

Yes   No   Number

4 UK property

If you received income from UK property (including rents and other income from land you own or lease out), read the notes to decide if you need to fill in the 'UK property' pages. You may not need to if this income is up to £1,000.
Do you need to fill in the 'UK property' pages?

Yes   No

5 Foreign

If you:
• were entitled to any foreign income
• have, or could have, received (directly or indirectly) income, or a capital payment or benefit from a person abroad as a result of any transfer of assets
• want to claim relief for foreign tax paid
read the notes to decide if you need to fill in the 'Foreign' pages. You may not need to if your only foreign income was from land and property abroad up to £1,000.
Do you need to fill in the 'Foreign' pages?

Yes   No

6 Trusts etc

Did you receive, or are you treated as having received, income from a trust, settlement or the residue of a deceased person's estate? This does not include cash lump sums/transfer of assets, otherwise known as capital distributions, received under a will.

Yes   No

7 Capital Gains Tax summary

If you sold or disposed of any assets (for example, stocks, shares, land and property, a business), or had any chargeable gains, read the notes to decide if you have to fill in the 'Capital Gains Tax summary' page.
If you do, you must also provide separate computations.
Do you need to fill in the 'Capital Gains Tax summary' page and provide computations?

Yes   No   Computation(s) provided

8 Residence, remittance basis etc

Were you, for all or part of the year to 5 April 2023, one or more of the following:
• not resident
• not domiciled in the UK and claiming the remittance basis
• dual resident in the UK and another country?

Yes   No

9 Additional information

Some less common kinds of income and tax reliefs, for example, Married Couple's Allowance, Life insurance gains, chargeable event gains, Seafarer's Earnings Deduction and details of disclosed tax avoidance schemes, should be returned on the 'Additional information' pages. Do you need to fill in the 'Additional information' pages?

Yes   No

If you need more pages

If you answered 'Yes' to any of questions 1 to 9, please check to see if within this return, there's a page dealing with that kind of income or gain.
If there's not, you'll need separate supplementary pages. Do you need to get and fill in separate supplementary pages?

Yes   No

If 'Yes', go to www.gov.uk/taxreturnforms to download them.

SA100 2023   Page TR 2

This page tells HMRC what sections of the tax return you have completed. This is particularly important for a paper return as several of the sections are independent forms which have to be attached if relevant. Note that this attachment happens automatically with filing online.

Section 3: Partnership – note that if you are self-employed in conjunction with someone else, you complete this section instead of the self-employment section.

You will also have to complete a Partnership return for the business as a whole. This return covers partnership income and expenses for the tax year ended 5 April. Your share of those profits is entered in the partnership section of the personal tax return. Therefore, it is probably best to complete the partnership return first, then you can transfer the relevant figures across to your personal tax return.

Section 8: Residence – as I have explained earlier, I am skirting around certain issues due to the size of UK tax law. There are various rules to determine if you are resident in the UK for tax purposes. This governs whether certain foreign income and capital gains incurred while living abroad are taxable in the UK.

If you have lived in the UK for the whole of the tax year, you don't need to worry about this section. It will be of more interest to those who will be living abroad and wish to arrange their affairs so as not to pay UK tax on foreign income and gains in that period.

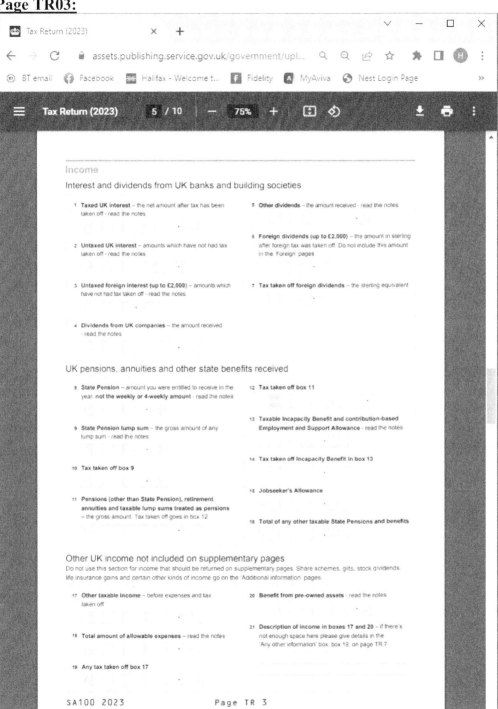

Income

Interest and dividends from UK banks and building societies

1 **Taxed UK interest** – the net amount after tax has been taken off - read the notes

2 **Untaxed UK interest** – amounts which have not had tax taken off - read the notes

3 **Untaxed foreign interest (up to £2,000)** – amounts which have not had tax taken off - read the notes

4 **Dividends from UK companies** – the amount received - read the notes

5 **Other dividends** – the amount received - read the notes

6 **Foreign dividends (up to £2,000)** – the amount in sterling after foreign tax was taken off. Do not include this amount in the 'Foreign' pages

7 **Tax taken off foreign dividends** – the sterling equivalent

UK pensions, annuities and other state benefits received

8 **State Pension** – amount you were entitled to receive in the year, **not the weekly or 4-weekly amount** - read the notes

9 **State Pension lump sum** – the gross amount of any lump sum - read the notes

10 **Tax taken off box 9**

11 **Pensions (other than State Pension), retirement annuities and taxable lump sums treated as pensions** – the gross amount. Tax taken off goes in box 12

12 **Tax taken off box 11**

13 **Taxable Incapacity Benefit and contribution-based Employment and Support Allowance** - read the notes

14 **Tax taken off Incapacity Benefit in box 13**

15 **Jobseeker's Allowance**

16 **Total of any other taxable State Pensions and benefits**

Other UK income not included on supplementary pages

Do not use this section for income that should be returned on supplementary pages. Share schemes, gifts, stock dividends, life insurance gains and certain other kinds of income go on the 'Additional information' pages.

17 **Other taxable income** – before expenses and tax taken off

18 **Total amount of allowable expenses** – read the notes

19 **Any tax taken off box 17**

20 **Benefit from pre-owned assets** - read the notes

21 **Description of income in boxes 17 and 20** – if there's not enough space here please give details in the 'Any other information' box, box 19, on page TR 7

SA100 2023   Page TR 3

Now we begin the pages where you record your taxable income.

There are three sections to this page:

Interest and dividends from UK banks, building societies:

Box 1 & 2: UK Interest – this will be the amount actually received in your bank account. Since the 6 April 2016 banks and building societies pay their interest gross, with no tax deducted at source, and so should mostly be entered in box 2. With the personal savings allowance you will not be due any tax on it, unless you exceed the amount of £1,000 for a basic rate tax payer or £500 for a higher rate tax payer.

Note that the interest entered in boxes 1 and 2 is the interest received in the tax year to 5 April. If you are self-employed, you may produce accounts with a different year end. These may show interest received in your business bank accounts during that accounting year. I would just point out that for these tax return boxes you will need to adjust this figure to the interest received in the tax year, even though you will be assessed on the self-employed income based on your accounting year.

You should also include interest received on any loans that you made to private individuals or any alternative funding arrangements you participated in, such as crowd funding.

Although interest that falls within the personal savings allowance is not taxable, it does count as part of your income for determining when the higher and upper rate tax thresholds are exceeded. If you have income that crosses those thresholds, you may need to complete a tax return to correct the tax paid which may otherwise have been deducted at source at a lower tax rate.

Boxes 4 & 5: Dividends – as with the interest received, you need to make sure that you enter the dividends which were paid within the tax year. Check the payment dates on the dividend vouchers.
If you did not receive dividend vouchers or have misplaced them, you may be able to find out the dividend rate and calculate the dividend based on your number of shares. This information would be available on the website of the

company in which you have shares. Probably the easiest method though would be to look up the amount received in your bank account.

Note that there are some special rules for Santander scrip dividends. If you have any of these shares you will probably have received documentation from the company regarding how your income should be treated. Alternatively, you might want to check the Santander website.

There is a tax-free allowance for dividends whereby you can receive £2,000 of dividends without paying tax. Above this, dividends are taxable at 8.75% for basic rate taxpayers and 33.75% for higher rate taxpayers. This allowance will be reducing in the 23/24 year to £1,000 and then again to £500 for the 24/25 tax year.

Company directors:
You might be a director-shareholder of a limited company. There are many individuals who operate their businesses with this structure. There are various pros and cons of operating through a limited company versus operating as a sole trader. It is one of those cases where you have to weigh up how different factors apply to your personal circumstances.
If you are a shareholder in your own company, you will report any dividends you have declared in the tax year in box 4.
I would advise you to create dividend vouchers and meeting minutes for your records. These will show that the dividends were official and were declared by the board of the company (even if you are its only member!).

UK pensions, annuities and other state benefits received:
Be careful to enter the amounts that you were due to receive in the tax year.
Due to timing differences this may be different to what you actually
received.

Note that Winter Fuel supplements are not taxable, so you do not need to
include them.
Likewise, there are some state benefits which will be taxable and others
which will not.

Taxable benefits include:
State pension
Jobseeker's allowance
Carer's allowance
Employment & support allowance (Contribution based)
Incapacity benefit
Bereavement allowance

Exempt benefits include:
Housing benefit
Employment & support allowance (income related)
Income support
Working tax credit
Child tax credit
Disability living allowance
Child benefit (income based)
Attendance allowance
Winter fuel supplement and Christmas bonus
Maternity allowance
Lump sum bereavement allowance
Universal credit

For the full and up to date list see the gov.uk website:
www.gov.uk/income-tax/taxfree-and-taxable-state-benefits

Box 9 is for the circumstance where you received a one-off lump sum from
the Department of Work and Pensions because you chose to put off or delay
claiming your state pension for at least 12 consecutive months.

Other UK income not included on supplementary pages:
This will include any miscellaneous income, which is not significant enough to be worth including on its own separate self-employment page. As the title suggests this is any other income that is not being recorded elsewhere on the tax return. The examples given by HMRC include casual earnings, commission, property income from a Real Estate Investment Trust and business receipts from a business that has ceased, such as bad debts recovered after a shop closed.

Other examples would be isolated literary or artistic activities, sale of patent rights, rent from the leasing of equipment that you own, personal insurance payments for sickness or injury, compensation (but not for redundancy or compensation for losing your job).

Note that you are allowed to record expenses against miscellaneous income as you would with self-employment.

Since 6 April 2017 there is a £1,000 exemption for other income before it becomes taxable. The government has said this is to provide a tax exemption for people making small sums of income, for example from an Air BNB rental. There is a £1,000 trading allowance and also a £1,000 allowance for property income, below which those forms of income are not taxable.

Badges of trade:
One thing I would note is that if you are doing something which is more of a hobby, in which you perhaps generally make more of a loss than a profit or in which you are never likely to make a profit, you should not report that. HMRC would take the view that such losses are not trading and therefore not available as tax relief.

Trading does not carry a statutory definition, but there is some guidance. Court cases have established what is known as the 'Badges of trade'. These are a series of factors which indicate that a transaction is trading and therefore taxable for income tax rather than being a capital transaction or exempt. If you have doubts about whether you have been trading or not, consider the following.
The badges are:
  1. Profit seeking motive – did you sell something with the intention of making a profit?
  2. Number of transactions – are they systematic and repeated?

3. Nature of asset sold – e.g. a picture held for personal enjoyment might not be trade if sold.

4. Existence of other similar trading transactions or interests.

5. Changes to the asset – was it repaired or improved to increase the sale value?

6. The way the sale was carried out – was it typical of trading or to raise cash in an emergency?

7. The source of the finance – was money borrowed to buy the asset that could only be repaid by selling the asset?

8. Interval time between purchase and sale – a short interval might indicate it was bought to sell.

9. Method of acquisition – a gift or inheritance is less likely to be the subject of trade.

Page TR04:

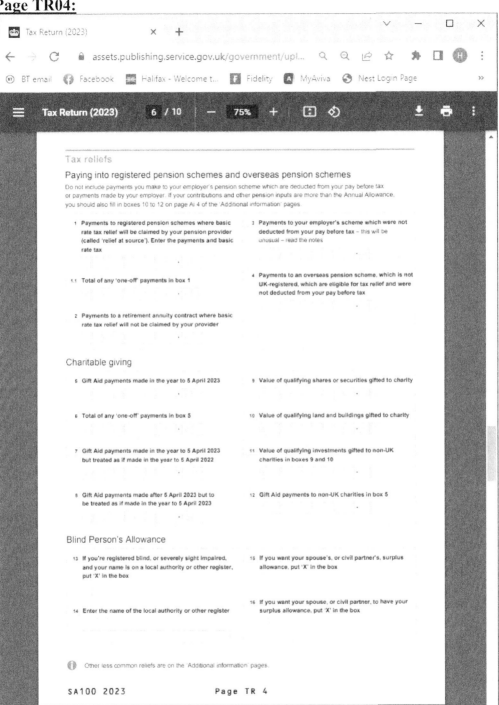

Tax reliefs

Paying into registered pension schemes and overseas pension schemes

Do not include payments you make to your employer's pension scheme which are deducted from your pay before tax or payments made by your employer. If your contributions and other pension inputs are more than the Annual Allowance, you should also fill in boxes 10 to 12 on page Ai 4 of the 'Additional information' pages.

1 Payments to registered pension schemes where basic rate tax relief will be claimed by your pension provider (called 'relief at source'). Enter the payments and basic rate tax

1.1 Total of any 'one-off' payments in box 1

2 Payments to a retirement annuity contract where basic rate tax relief will not be claimed by your provider

3 Payments to your employer's scheme which were not deducted from your pay before tax – this will be unusual – read the notes

4 Payments to an overseas pension scheme, which is not UK-registered, which are eligible for tax relief and were not deducted from your pay before tax

Charitable giving

5 Gift Aid payments made in the year to 5 April 2023

6 Total of any 'one-off' payments in box 5

7 Gift Aid payments made in the year to 5 April 2023 but treated as if made in the year to 5 April 2022

8 Gift Aid payments made after 5 April 2023 but to be treated as if made in the year to 5 April 2023

9 Value of qualifying shares or securities gifted to charity

10 Value of qualifying land and buildings gifted to charity

11 Value of qualifying investments gifted to non-UK charities in boxes 9 and 10

12 Gift Aid payments to non-UK charities in box 5

Blind Person's Allowance

13 If you're registered blind, or severely sight impaired, and your name is on a local authority or other register, put 'X' in the box

14 Enter the name of the local authority or other register

15 If you want your spouse's, or civil partner's, surplus allowance, put 'X' in the box

16 If you want your spouse, or civil partner, to have your surplus allowance, put 'X' in the box

Other less common reliefs are on the 'Additional information' pages.

SA100 2023   Page TR 4

Here you get to report two common reliefs which will potentially reduce your tax liability.

Paying into registered pension schemes and overseas pensions schemes: This includes any payments to personal pension schemes made by yourself. It will not include any payments made by your employer or your limited company if you are a director or shareholder in a company. In those situations, tax relief is achieved in other ways.

The amount contributed to a personal pension scheme will extend the basic rate band by the gross amount of the contributions in the tax year. That is the amount paid x 100/80.

Under an employer scheme the 20% which would have been taxed under PAYE before you received it is returned to you through a government contribution to your pension, claimed by your pension provider.

Under current rules you can make a pension contribution of £40,000 in one year. If you exceed this, you could be liable to a tax charge (In the March 2023 budget it was announced that this will be increasing to £60,000 on 6 April 2023).

Charitable giving:
Gift aid payments have the same effect as pensions in that they extend your basic rate band, increasing the amount of income you can receive before paying higher rate tax.

However, there is a hidden pitfall; if you have not paid enough tax in the year, a liability will result from the gift aid payment, equivalent to the amount paid to the charity by the government. This can result where all of your income falls within the personal allowance and therefore no tax would otherwise be due. It could be an increasing issue where individuals with low incomes supplement their PAYE income with an investment in dividends or bank interest, because the dividend and personal savings allowances mean no tax being due on the first £2,000 and £1,000 from those sources respectively.

You can ask for Gift aid payments to be applied to the previous tax year provided you do so before you have filed your tax return for the year before.

There are some circumstances where donations of goods can be gift aided. When goods qualify, they fall under the same rules as the donation of cash. There are two specific boxes (9 and 10) for the gifting of shares and of land & buildings to charity.

23

Page TR05:

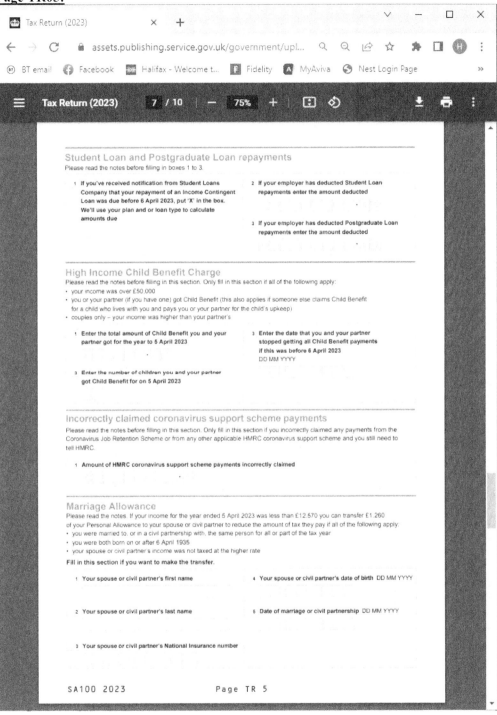

Student Loan and Postgraduate Loan repayments

Please read the notes before filling in boxes 1 to 3.

1 If you've received notification from Student Loans Company that your repayment of an Income Contingent Loan was due before 6 April 2023, put 'X' in the box. We'll use your plan and or loan type to calculate amounts due

2 If your employer has deducted Student Loan repayments enter the amount deducted

3 If your employer has deducted Postgraduate Loan repayments enter the amount deducted

High Income Child Benefit Charge

Please read the notes before filling in this section. Only fill in this section if all of the following apply:

- your income was over £50,000
- you or your partner (if you have one) got Child Benefit (this also applies if someone else claims Child Benefit for a child who lives with you and pays you or your partner for the child's upkeep)
- couples only – your income was higher than your partner's

1 Enter the total amount of Child Benefit you and your partner got for the year to 5 April 2023

3 Enter the date that you and your partner stopped getting all Child Benefit payments if this was before 6 April 2023
DD MM YYYY

3 Enter the number of children you and your partner got Child Benefit for on 5 April 2023

Incorrectly claimed coronavirus support scheme payments

Please read the notes before filling in this section. Only fill in this section if you incorrectly claimed any payments from the Coronavirus Job Retention Scheme or from any other applicable HMRC coronavirus support scheme and you still need to tell HMRC.

1 Amount of HMRC coronavirus support scheme payments incorrectly claimed

Marriage Allowance

Please read the notes. If your income for the year ended 5 April 2023 was less than £12,570 you can transfer £1,260 of your Personal Allowance to your spouse or civil partner to reduce the amount of tax they pay if all of the following apply:

- you were married to, or in a civil partnership with, the same person for all or part of the tax year
- you were both born on or after 6 April 1935
- your spouse or civil partner's income was not taxed at the higher rate

Fill in this section if you want to make the transfer.

1 Your spouse or civil partner's first name

4 Your spouse or civil partner's date of birth DD MM YYYY

2 Your spouse or civil partner's last name

5 Date of marriage or civil partnership DD MM YYYY

3 Your spouse or civil partner's National Insurance number

24

This page covers three special categories which may affect your tax liability.

Student Loan Repayments – you will be able to see from your payslip whether student loan repayments have been deducted from your salary. It is important to enter them here so HMRC understands why your taxable pay is lower than they might otherwise expect.
Income based or income contingent loans are repaid through the tax system. These were introduced in 1998.

From 6 April 2022 the income threshold to make loan repayments is £20,195 for plan 1 loans, £27,295 for plan 2 loans, £25,375 for plan 4 loans, £25,000 for Plan 5 loans, and £21,000 for postgraduate loans.

High Income Child Benefit Charge – in this book I am assuming that you have relatively simple tax affairs, but it is still possible that you have a partner with a high paid job or that you yourself are a higher earner, even though you have relatively few other income sources.

If you earn over £50,000, then you will need to record the amount of child benefit that you or your partner received in the tax year. Where one of you earns over this amount, there is a clawback of the child benefit received. At £60,000 all child benefit is recovered; between these two thresholds a proportion is withdrawn (1% of the child benefit for every £100 of income over £50,000).

Marriage allowance – Under this allowance if you are married or in a civil partnership and one of you earns less than the personal allowance, whilst the other is not a higher rate taxpayer, you can make an separate election online to transfer 10% of the lower taxpayer's personal allowance to the other. This could save up to £252 in tax.

To avoid any confusion, there is another married couples' allowance which is included on the tax return, but this is only claimable where one of the people in the marriage or civil partnership was born before 6 April 1935. This appears in the additional information section of the tax return.

Page TR06:

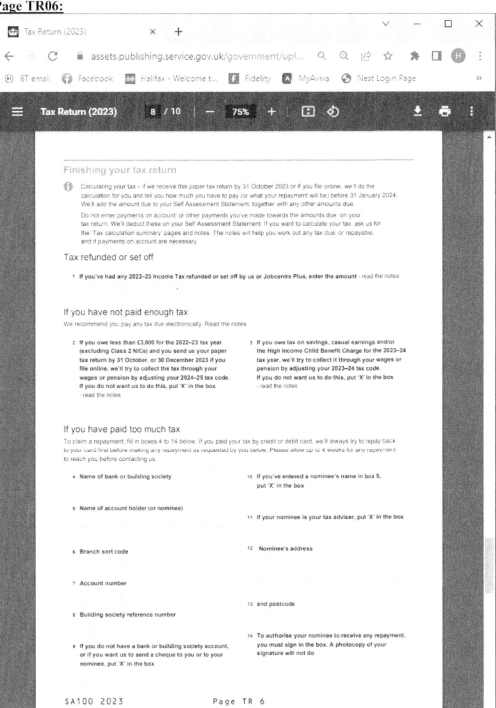

Finishing your tax return

ℹ️ Calculating your tax – if we receive this paper tax return by 31 October 2023 or if you file online, we'll do the calculation for you and tell you how much you have to pay (or what your repayment will be) before 31 January 2024. We'll add the amount due to your Self Assessment Statement, together with any other amounts due.

Do not enter payments on account, or other payments you've made towards the amounts due, on your tax return. We'll deduct these on your Self Assessment Statement. If you want to calculate your tax, ask us for the 'Tax calculation summary' pages and notes. The notes will help you work out any tax due, or repayable, and if payments on account are necessary.

Tax refunded or set off

1 If you've had any 2022–23 Income Tax refunded or set off by us or Jobcentre Plus, enter the amount - read the notes

If you have not paid enough tax

We recommend you pay any tax due electronically. Read the notes.

2 If you owe less than £3,000 for the 2022–23 tax year (excluding Class 2 NICs) and you send us your paper tax return by 31 October, or 30 December 2023 if you file online, we'll try to collect the tax through your wages or pension by adjusting your 2024–25 tax code. If you do not want us to do this, put 'X' in the box - read the notes

3 If you owe tax on savings, casual earnings and/or the High Income Child Benefit Charge for the 2023–24 tax year, we'll try to collect it through your wages or pension by adjusting your 2023–24 tax code. If you do not want us to do this, put 'X' in the box - read the notes

If you have paid too much tax

To claim a repayment, fill in boxes 4 to 14 below. If you paid your tax by credit or debit card, we'll always try to repay back to your card first before making any repayment as requested by you below. Please allow up to 4 weeks for any repayment to reach you before contacting us.

4 Name of bank or building society

5 Name of account holder (or nominee)

6 Branch sort code

7 Account number

8 Building society reference number

9 If you do not have a bank or building society account, or if you want us to send a cheque to you or to your nominee, put 'X' in the box

10 If you've entered a nominee's name in box 5, put 'X' in the box

11 If your nominee is your tax adviser, put 'X' in the box

12 Nominee's address

13 and postcode

14 To authorise your nominee to receive any repayment, you must sign in the box. A photocopy of your signature will not do

SA100 2023   Page TR 6

This page concerns some options if you have additional tax to pay or if a refund is due.

There is a section here where you can record your bank details. If you have completed this and are due a refund, it will be transferred to your bank account once the tax return has been processed by HMRC. Otherwise, they will send you a cheque.
This may include interest at the official rate if they have held your money beyond the payment deadline, for example if you file an amended return and it turns out you owe less tax than previously expected.

On the other hand, you may have a tax liability.
If you are paid wages by an employer or a pension, you can choose to code out a liability of less than £3,000. This means you don't have to send a payment to HMRC. Instead, they will alter your tax code for a future year, such that the additional tax will be deducted from your net wages or pension income over the course of that year.

Note that this happens by default, so if you don't want it to happen take care to tick the appropriate boxes under the 'If you have not paid enough tax' section.

Should you have coded out a liability from a previous tax year, such that your tax code was adjusted for this year, then you need to enter that liability in box 1 on this page. In that way HMRC will know why you have paid extra PAYE during the year.

 Finally, in order to code out a tax liability you will need to file a paper return by 31 October or an electronic return by 30 December.

Page TR07:

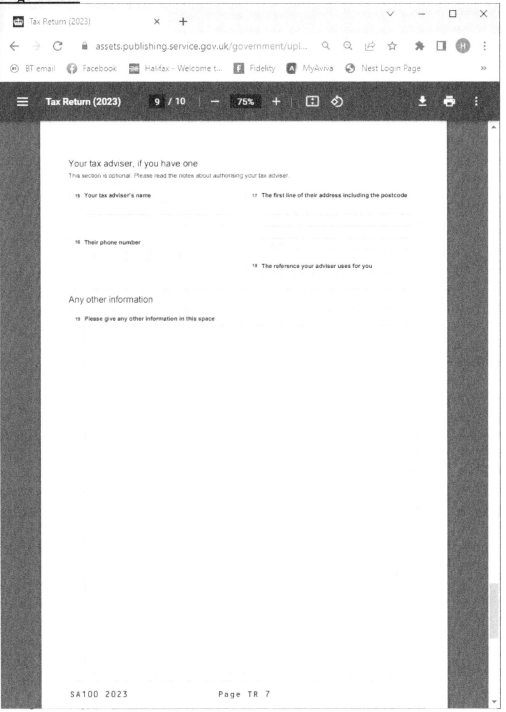

Your tax adviser, if you have one

This section is optional. Please read the notes about authorising your tax adviser.

15 Your tax adviser's name

16 Their phone number

17 The first line of their address including the postcode

18 The reference your adviser uses for you

Any other information

19 Please give any other information in this space

28

Boxes 15-18: These would be filled in if a tax adviser were completing your return for you. Since this book is about filing your own tax return, I will not refer to these entries further.

Box 19 'Any Other Information':

Here you can draw attention to anything you feel needs to be highlighted to HMRC. Examples might be: what makes up capital introduced into the business by a self-employed person or a breakdown of which pension providers you received pensions from. Basically, any areas where there is not space to include enough detail on the rest of the form – although you should make sure the total figures are recorded elsewhere on the form, even if you are breaking them down here. This is where you would also note if you were part of a tax avoidance scheme. If so, you would have received a scheme reference number from the organiser of the scheme and would note it here.

Page TR08:

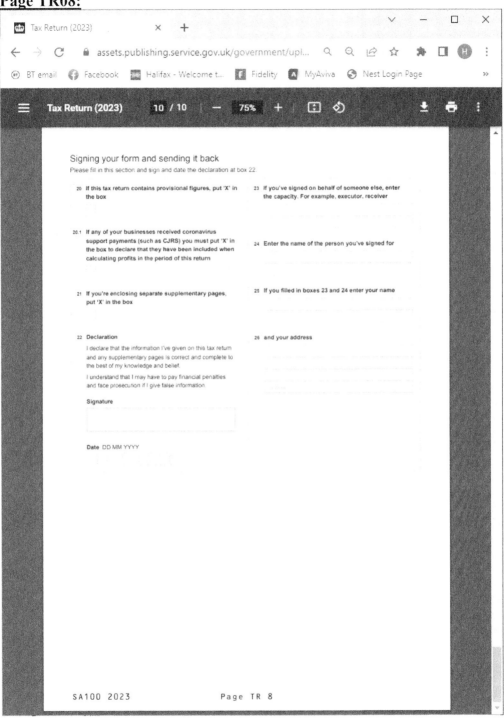

Signing your form and sending it back

Please fill in this section and sign and date the declaration at box 22.

20 If this tax return contains provisional figures, put 'X' in the box

20.1 If any of your businesses received coronavirus support payments (such as CJRS) you must put 'X' in the box to declare that they have been included when calculating profits in the period of this return

21 If you're enclosing separate supplementary pages, put 'X' in the box

22 Declaration

I declare that the information I've given on this tax return and any supplementary pages is correct and complete to the best of my knowledge and belief.

I understand that I may have to pay financial penalties and face prosecution if I give false information.

Signature

Date DD MM YYYY

23 If you've signed on behalf of someone else, enter the capacity. For example, executor, receiver

24 Enter the name of the person you've signed for

25 If you filled in boxes 23 and 24 enter your name

26 and your address

30

This is the last page of the main tax return.

Box 20: Provisional or estimated figures:
The deadline for filing a tax return online is 31 January following the end of the tax year.
You then have a year following that date to submit an amended return.
Under exceptional circumstances should you be unable to give full details of your tax circumstances by the January deadline, you can choose to enter estimated figures for your income and expenses, which you would then revise with a subsequent amending return.
If you are putting in estimated figures, you should put an X in **Box 20**.

Box 21: Supplemental pages:
If you have to fill out forms for other types of income not covered in the main return, such as capital gains, self-employment, employment or rental income, then you need to put a cross in this box.
The same would be true if you were filing a paper return and had to attach additional pages because you ran out of space in one of the previous sections, for example the additional information box.

You will see **Boxes 23-26** concern the circumstance that you are signing the return on behalf of someone else.

Box 22 - declaration:
This is one of the most important bits. If you are filing a paper return, you must sign and date this in order to indicate that the information you have supplied is correct as far as you are aware.
If you are filing electronically, you will find that pressing a button to submit the return is deemed to have the same function.

You should make sure that the figures you have supplied are as accurate as possible to the extent of your knowledge, because HMRC can levy fines or penalties for errors in a tax return resulting from carelessness.
If you become aware of a mistake that you think is material, you can file an amending return within a year of the original deadline.
HMRC can enquire into a return filed on time within 12 months of receiving it. If filed late, they have until the quarter day following the first anniversary of the actual filing date (where the quarter days are 31 January, 30 April, 31 July and 31 October).

Where a tax return has been amended after the original filing deadline, the deadline for an enquiry is the same as for a late return.

HMRC also have powers to go back further than this in certain circumstances. For example, where fraud is suspected, they can go back up to 20 years.

33

Supplemental pages:

Capital Gains Tax Summary – form SA108:

A capital gain can result when you dispose of property. Common types of property for this tax are stocks & shares, land & buildings and business assets.

If you are still unsure of what a capital gain is, it is the surplus that results from the sale of an asset, taking into account your original acquisition costs, any incidental costs of purchase or sale, net of your capital gains tax annual exemption.

One useful exemption is Private Residence Relief. This effectively means that if you only own one property and you have lived there the whole time you owned it, you will not need to pay capital gains tax when you sell the property.

A disposal can occur when an asset is sold, but also when it is given away, exchanged or destroyed.

Connected persons:

One special case of a disposal is when an asset is given away to a connected person. Here the market value of the asset is used as the proceeds in working out the capital gain.

Connected persons include brothers and sisters, parents or grandparents, spouses or civil partners of the above, or a company that you control (but note that there is a spousal exemption where a spouse is treated as receiving the asset on a no-gain no-loss basis. That means their acquisition cost is effectively the original cost of the asset).

Calculating capital gains:

One example of a capital gains calculation would be in the sale of a rental property.

The amount you received for it, net of legal costs of sale would be the proceeds of the sale.

The original purchase price would be the cost, plus cost of any improvement works on the property, for example adding an extension, plus again legal fees involved in making the purchase.

After subtracting the cost from the proceeds, you would be left with the capital gain.

For any given tax year, there is an annual exemption, which for 2022/23 currently stands at £12,300. (It will be reduced to £6,000 for the 5 April 2024 tax year and then again down to £3,000 for the 5 April 2025 tax year). After subtracting this from your total capital gains, you would arrive at your taxable income. Capital gains on residential property are currently taxed at 18% for basic rate taxpayers and 28% for higher rate. Note that you have to take into account your other income that year to find out if or how much of a gain falls into the higher rate threshold.

Since 6 April 2016 capital gains on other types of income are taxed at 10% for basic rate taxpayers or 20% for higher rate taxpayers.

You are required to attach your calculations of the capital gains recorded to your tax return.

Page CG01:

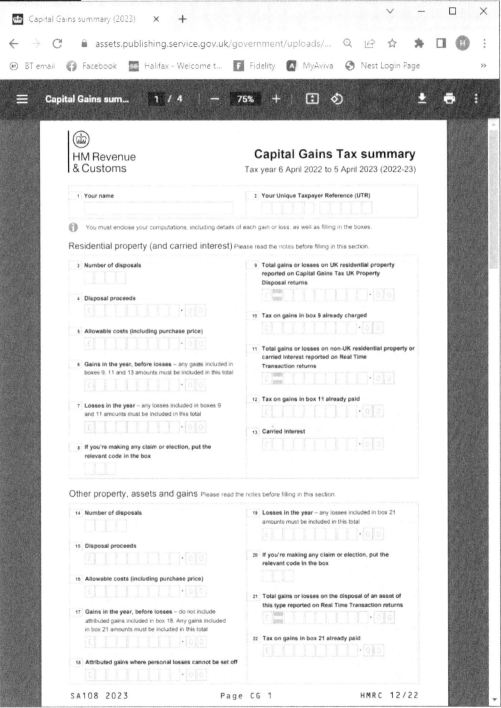

As with all of the supplemental sections of the tax return, this begins with a box for your name and one for the Unique Taxpayer Reference which you would have looked up to go on the main form. This is from the days when paper returns were the norm and loose pages could potentially have become separated from the whole.

HMRC provides a helpsheet, which you can use to work out your capital gains before entering them on the form. As noted above, you have to include a copy of your calculations with the form you submit. One possibility would be to enter them in the other information Box 54 on page CG4. The accounting software I use attaches a separate sheet. If your software does not do this, another option could be to attach a scanned in copy of the calculations on the helpsheet.

Some notes:

Although I don't propose to write a thorough manual on Capital Gains Tax here, it will be worth highlighting a few points:

1. Motor cars are not subject to capital gains tax.
2. Some other assets are specifically exempted, including personal effects of value up to £6,000, premium bonds, UK government stocks and government investment schemes such as Enterprise Investment Scheme and Venture Capital Trust shares.
3. Transfers between spouses are also exempt.
4. If you dispose of your home and have never rented it out or used it as business premises, then it will be covered by Private Residence Relief and no capital gains tax will be due.
5. When it comes to physical things that can be moved around, there are some thresholds before those things become taxable. These are called the chattels rules. See the next box.

Chattels rules:

Chattels include:

Items of household furniture

Paintings, antiques, items of crockery and china

Motor vehicles

Items of plant and machinery not permanently attached to a building

But: Motor cars are exempt from capital gains tax as are chattels with a limited lifespan.

With a chattel you only need to register a gain if the proceeds you received were more than £6,000.

If your proceeds were between £6,001 and £15,000 the gain is limited to:
5/3 x (Proceeds - £6,000)

In other words, calculate the gain and if it is higher than the results of the above formula, then the gain is equal to those results.

If there is a loss and the proceeds are less than £6,000, the loss is restricted by treating the disposal proceeds as £6,000.

Capital loss relief
The other point worth noting on this page is that you will see that there is a box (7) for losses. Capital losses can be carried forward to offset against future gains. Therefore, if you make a loss of this nature, you could find it worthwhile to include it in your tax return to offset against a gain which you might make in a future year.

Loss relief is another complicated area, but I will try to touch on a few key points.
A capital loss can be offset against capital gains in the same tax year (you may have gains on disposal of some assets and losses on others). If there is a net loss, it can be carried forward to offset against future capital gains.
If a loss brought forward is set against a gain in the current year, use of that loss is restricted to the amount that reduces the gain to the annual exemption for capital gains – in other words the annual exemption is preserved.
Capital losses cannot be set against other taxable income except in very limited circumstances which I will not go into here.

Box 6: is where you enter the total gains.
Box 7: is where you enter the total losses.

Boxes 8 & 20: this is where you put codes relating to different types of relief you might be claiming. Private Residence Relief would be one example, Business Asset Disposal relief is another. Business Asset Disposal relief potentially applies on disposal of a business that you have been running and if it applies the capital gain is taxed at the lower rate of 10%.

Qualifying for Business Asset Disposal Relief (formerly called Entrepreneur's relief):

Business Asset Disposal relief applies if you have disposed of:
1. All or part of your business as a sole trader or business partner
2. Shares or securities in a company where you have at least 5% of shares and voting rights.
3. Assets you lent to your business or personal company.

If you are selling all or part of your business the following must apply:
1. You must be a sole trader or business partner
2. You must have owned the business at least two years before you sell it or close it down.
3. You must dispose of the business assets within 3 years.

If you are selling shares the following must apply:
1. You must be an employee or office holder of the company for at least two years before sale of the shares (the years leading up to the sale).
2. The company must be a trading company rather than holding investments.

This relief can also be available for the disposal of assets associated with the business under some circumstances:
1. You must have sold at least 5% of your interest or shares in the business.
2. The business must have had use of the asset/s for at least a year before the sale or closure of the business.

Page CG02:

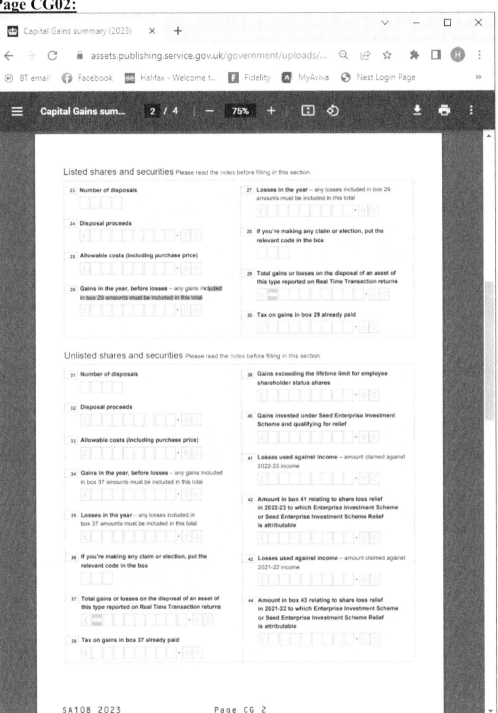

Listed shares and securities Please read the notes before filling in this section.

23 Number of disposals

24 Disposal proceeds
£ . 0 0

25 Allowable costs (including purchase price)
£ . 0 0

26 Gains in the year, before losses – any gains included in box 29 amounts must be included in this total
£ . 0 0

27 Losses in the year – any losses included in box 29 amounts must be included in this total
£ . 0 0

28 If you're making any claim or election, put the relevant code in the box

29 Total gains or losses on the disposal of an asset of this type reported on Real Time Transaction returns
£ . 0 0

30 Tax on gains in box 29 already paid
£ . 0 0

Unlisted shares and securities Please read the notes before filling in this section.

31 Number of disposals

32 Disposal proceeds
£ . 0 0

33 Allowable costs (including purchase price)
£ . 0 0

34 Gains in the year, before losses – any gains included in box 37 amounts must be included in this total
£ . 0 0

35 Losses in the year – any losses included in box 37 amounts must be included in this total
£ . 0 0

36 If you're making any claim or election, put the relevant code in the box

37 Total gains or losses on the disposal of an asset of this type reported on Real Time Transaction returns
£ . 0 0

38 Tax on gains in box 37 already paid
£ . 0 0

39 Gains exceeding the lifetime limit for employee shareholder status shares
£ . 0 0

40 Gains invested under Seed Enterprise Investment Scheme and qualifying for relief
£ . 0 0

41 Losses used against income – amount claimed against 2022-23 income
£ . 0 0

42 Amount in box 41 relating to share loss relief in 2022-23 to which Enterprise Investment Scheme or Seed Enterprise Investment Scheme Relief is attributable
£ . 0 0

43 Losses used against income – amount claimed against 2021-22 income
£ . 0 0

44 Amount in box 43 relating to share loss relief in 2021-22 to which Enterprise Investment Scheme or Seed Enterprise Investment Scheme Relief is attributable
£ . 0 0

Listed shares and securities:
If you have an investment portfolio with a broker, they should provide you with a tax certificate which will show the number of disposals, the disposal proceeds and capital gains.

Likewise, an investment in a particular quoted shareholding that is disposed of should mean that a tax certificate is sent to you.

Unlisted shares and securities:
In this section you would enter any capital gains from shares and securities not listed on a stock exchange. One example would be the disposal of shares in a limited company that you had set up as a vehicle for a business that you were running.

Each of these sections include a box whereby claims and elections affecting capital gains tax can be entered (**Boxes 28 and 36**). For quoted shares there is a relief called negligible value relief. This is available where you bought some shares which no longer have any value, for example in a company which has gone into administration since you acquired the shares. If it applies it would effectively create a capital loss equal to the original purchase price of the shares.

Page CG03:

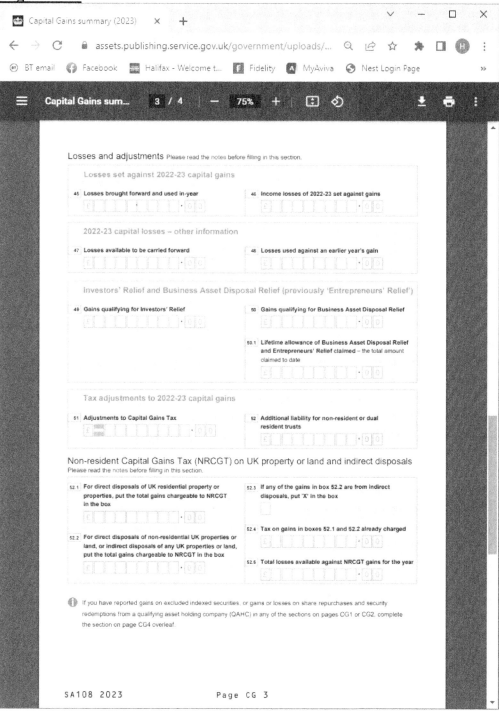

Losses and adjustments Please read the notes before filling in this section.

Losses set against 2022-23 capital gains

45 Losses brought forward and used in-year

46 Income losses of 2022-23 set against gains

2022-23 capital losses – other information

47 Losses available to be carried forward

48 Losses used against an earlier year's gain

Investors' Relief and Business Asset Disposal Relief (previously 'Entrepreneurs' Relief')

49 Gains qualifying for Investors' Relief

50 Gains qualifying for Business Asset Disposal Relief

50.1 Lifetime allowance of Business Asset Disposal Relief and Entrepreneurs' Relief claimed – the total amount claimed to date

Tax adjustments to 2022-23 capital gains

51 Adjustments to Capital Gains Tax

52 Additional liability for non-resident or dual resident trusts

Non-resident Capital Gains Tax (NRCGT) on UK property or land and indirect disposals
Please read the notes before filling in this section.

52.1 For direct disposals of UK residential property or properties, put the total gains chargeable to NRCGT in the box

52.3 If any of the gains in box 52.2 are from indirect disposals, put 'X' in the box

52.2 For direct disposals of non-residential UK properties or land, or indirect disposals of any UK properties or land, put the total gains chargeable to NRCGT in the box

52.4 Tax on gains in boxes 52.1 and 52.2 already charged

52.5 Total losses available against NRCGT gains for the year

If you have reported gains on excluded indexed securities, or gains or losses on share repurchases and security redemptions from a qualifying asset holding company (QAHC) in any of the sections on pages CG1 or CG2, complete the section on page CG4 overleaf.

SA108 2023   Page CG 3

42

This page is where you list losses brought forward from previous years and any remaining losses after setting against gains in the year, which you can then carry forward.

If you are claiming Business Asset Disposal relief (formerly entrepreneur's relief), in addition to the boxes you completed on page CG01 or CG02, you also need to enter the gain on **Box 50** on this page.

Page CG04:

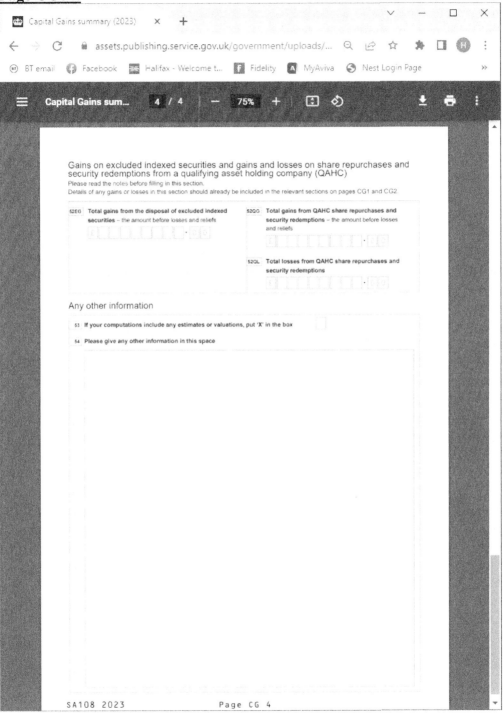

Gains on excluded indexed securities and gains and losses on share repurchases and security redemptions from a qualifying asset holding company (QAHC)

Please read the notes before filling in this section.

Details of any gains or losses in this section should already be included in the relevant sections on pages CG1 and CG2.

52EG Total gains from the disposal of excluded indexed securities – the amount before losses and reliefs

52QG Total gains from QAHC share repurchases and security redemptions – the amount before losses and reliefs

52QL Total losses from QAHC share repurchases and security redemptions

Any other information

53 If your computations include any estimates or valuations, put 'X' in the box

54 Please give any other information in this space

44

This last page of the capital gains section is for you to include any additional information that may be needed to understand what you have entered elsewhere on the form.

As I said earlier, it could be the place to show your calculations of capital gains.

UK Property – form SA105:

Page UKP1:

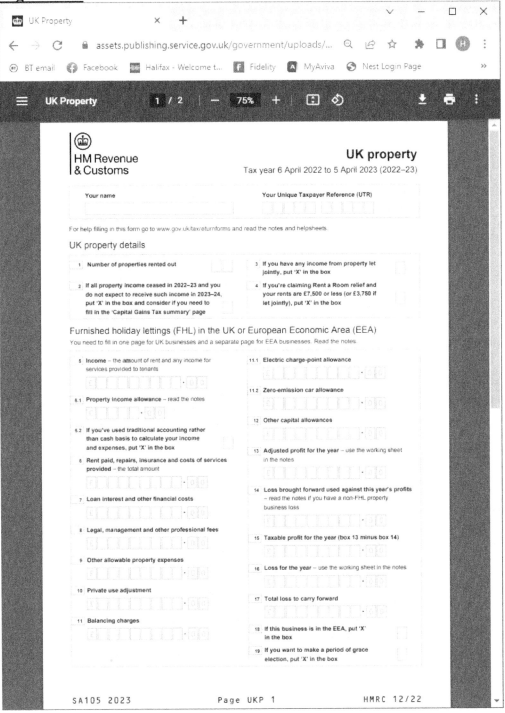

HM Revenue & Customs

UK property

Tax year 6 April 2022 to 5 April 2023 (2022–23)

Your name

Your Unique Taxpayer Reference (UTR)

For help filling in this form go to www.gov.uk/taxreturnforms and read the notes and helpsheets.

UK property details

1. Number of properties rented out

2. If all property income ceased in 2022–23 and you do not expect to receive such income in 2023–24, put 'X' in the box and consider if you need to fill in the 'Capital Gains Tax summary' page

3. If you have any income from property let jointly, put 'X' in the box

4. If you're claiming Rent a Room relief and your rents are £7,500 or less (or £3,750 if let jointly), put 'X' in the box

Furnished holiday lettings (FHL) in the UK or European Economic Area (EEA)

You need to fill in one page for UK businesses and a separate page for EEA businesses. Read the notes.

5. Income – the amount of rent and any income for services provided to tenants

5.1 Property income allowance – read the notes

5.2 If you've used traditional accounting rather than cash basis to calculate your income and expenses, put 'X' in the box

6. Rent paid, repairs, insurance and costs of services provided – the total amount

7. Loan interest and other financial costs

8. Legal, management and other professional fees

9. Other allowable property expenses

10. Private use adjustment

11. Balancing charges

11.1 Electric charge-point allowance

11.2 Zero-emission car allowance

12. Other capital allowances

13. Adjusted profit for the year – use the working sheet in the notes

14. Loss brought forward used against this year's profits – read the notes if you have a non-FHL property business loss

15. Taxable profit for the year (box 13 minus box 14)

16. Loss for the year – use the working sheet in the notes

17. Total loss to carry forward

18. If this business is in the EEA, put 'X' in the box

19. If you want to make a period of grace election, put 'X' in the box

SA105 2023   Page UKP 1   HMRC 12/22

This part of the tax return is for rental income from property. Running a hotel or guesthouse would be income from self-employment and would be recorded in that section.

Wayleaves (payments for access to land) are recorded as other income if they relate to land not used in your trade, or in the self-employment section if they relate to land used in your trade. A common example of the latter would be farmland.

AirBNB rental is relatively new form of property rental. For the current tax year (5 April 2023) you can report your income from AirBNB in one of two ways. If you rent out a room within your property, you can claim for rent a room relief (see more detail below). This means that if the rental income is less than £7,500 in total, you do not have to pay tax on it.

If you rent out a whole property, you will have to report the income as a residential let, recording all of your expenses and paying tax on your rental profits.

Since 6 April 2017, there is a £1,000 allowance for property and trading income, below which no tax will be due. A person who makes small sums on an AirBNB rental is one example given by the government as to whom this exemption will apply.

There are three main types of rental property: commercial lets, residential lets and furnished holiday lets.

Furnished holiday lets:

Furnished holiday lets are a specialised form of residential lets. If a property fulfils certain requirements for number of days available for rent and number of days actually rented, then it can qualify as a furnished holiday let. This gives the advantage that capital allowances can be claimed for the holiday let as though it were a trade.

In order to qualify as a furnished holiday let, a property must be in the UK or European Economic Area and:

(a) must be available for letting for 210 or more days in the year and

(b) must be actually let for 105 days or more in the year.

There are also restrictions on the long term lets (letting to the same tenant/s for an extended period) that are permitted, where a long term let is defined as 31-155 days. If the total of all the long term lets in the year exceeds 155 days, then the property will not qualify as a furnished holiday let.

Box 19: Period of grace election:

As already noted, there are conditions which a property must comply with in order to be a furnished holiday let. A period of grace is a concession allowing a property not to qualify for a brief period of time, yet still remain classified as a furnished holiday let.

This allows you to treat a year as a qualifying furnished holiday let year, where you genuinely intended to meet the occupancy threshold, but were unable to. The business must have qualified the year before.

You can make a period of grace election two years running, however the third year the business fails to meet the furnished holiday let requirements, the property will cease to be a furnished holiday let. That is to say, the business must qualify in year 1, then years 2 and 3 can be covered by the election, but then in year 4 it must qualify again.

Residential lets:

Residential lets can be rented unfurnished or furnished.

You cannot claim expenses for the initial cost of white goods such as a fridge, but you can claim for the costs of replacing an existing appliance. Note that the replacement cost will be restricted where there is an element of improvement, for example a washing machine being replaced by a washer dryer. In that case only the cost of an equivalent washing machine would be claimable.

Repairs on the building itself and small tools used in its maintenance are allowable costs.

The government has introduced measures to make the ownership of rental properties less palatable, in order to free up more homes for those who wish to buy them to live in. These include 3% additional stamp duty which applies to the purchase of second homes.

A second major measure, which was phased in from 6 April 2017, is the restriction of mortgage interest for landlords of rental properties. Now that this has been fully implemented, only basic rate tax relief is claimable against rental income for the mortgage interest charged. In the tax calculation, mortgage interest and finance charges will be disallowed, with a tax deduction brought in at the end, equal to 20% times the mortgage interest. If your total income is within the basic rate band before deduction of the mortgage interest from your rental income, you will not pay any additional tax because of this.

Most of the boxes on this page are self-explanatory, so I will only touch on them briefly.

Box 4: Rent a room relief:
If you let out a furnished room in your home and the total rental income is less than £7,500, or £3,750 if let jointly, then put a cross in **Box 4**.

If your rental income from this source is more than those limits, you can choose between paying tax just on the excess over the limits (put total income in **Box 20** and the exempt amount of £7,500 / £3,750 in **Box 37,** both boxes appearing on page UKP2) or on your net profit, taking into account all your rental income and any expenses you may have incurred in relation to the letting. In the latter case, the income is entered in **Box 20** and the expenses in **Boxes 24-29** (on page UKP2).

Box 10: Private usage adjustment:
If you rent out property, you must only claim for the business proportion of an expense and likewise you can adjust your taxable income to remove any proportion that represents private enjoyment of that income (this same rule applies for the business expenses of a self-employed person).

A common example for income would be the owner of a shop who might consume some of his own produce. For expenses, you might reduce fuel expenses for the proportion you estimate to be private journeys.

This section also includes the option to enter losses.
A loss in a UK furnished holiday let business can only be carried forward to set against a profit in the same UK furnished holiday let business – and if you have a UK and a foreign furnished holiday let, a loss in one cannot be set against a profit in the other.

Commercial lets:
Commercial lets are similar to residential lets, except that they would usually be rented unfurnished. They would include rental of a shop, garage or lockup.

51

Page UKP2:

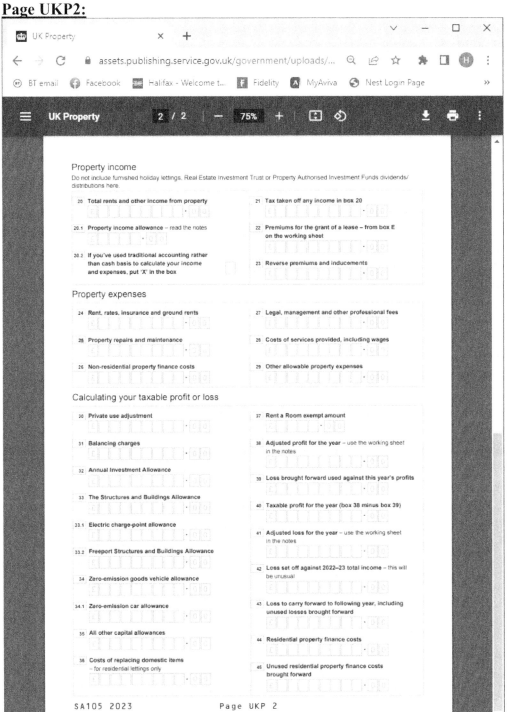

Property income

Do not include furnished holiday lettings, Real Estate Investment Trust or Property Authorised Investment Funds dividends/distributions here.

20 Total rents and other income from property

20.1 Property income allowance – read the notes

20.2 If you've used traditional accounting rather than cash basis to calculate your income and expenses, put 'X' in the box

21 Tax taken off any income in box 20

22 Premiums for the grant of a lease – from box E on the working sheet

23 Reverse premiums and inducements

Property expenses

24 Rent, rates, insurance and ground rents

25 Property repairs and maintenance

26 Non-residential property finance costs

27 Legal, management and other professional fees

28 Costs of services provided, including wages

29 Other allowable property expenses

Calculating your taxable profit or loss

30 Private use adjustment

31 Balancing charges

32 Annual Investment Allowance

33 The Structures and Buildings Allowance

33.1 Electric charge-point allowance

33.2 Freeport Structures and Buildings Allowance

34 Zero-emission goods vehicle allowance

34.1 Zero-emission car allowance

35 All other capital allowances

36 Costs of replacing domestic items – for residential lettings only

37 Rent a Room exempt amount

38 Adjusted profit for the year – use the working sheet in the notes

39 Loss brought forward used against this year's profits

40 Taxable profit for the year (box 38 minus box 39)

41 Adjusted loss for the year – use the working sheet in the notes

42 Loss set off against 2022–23 total income – this will be unusual

43 Loss to carry forward to following year, including unused losses brought forward

44 Residential property finance costs

45 Unused residential property finance costs brought forward

SA105 2023   Page UKP 2

52

Here the property section moves on to income from regular rental properties.

Box 25: Property repairs & maintenance:
In order to be allowable, amounts spent on the property must be repairs not replacement or upgrade of existing goods. Repainting and repairs to the building will usually qualify, but other work on the property will need to be evaluated to assess its deductibility. For example, replacing a kitchen could be repairs if it restores it to a condition that it was previously in, but not if it upgrades the kitchen somehow.
Purchase of small tools is also generally considered to be allowable.

Box 27: Legal, management and other professional fees:
Fees charged by a letting or management agent are allowable.
Make sure you record these according to the date the charge covers, not when the rent was received – e.g. rent for the month of March, but not received in the bank until after 5th April would still be recorded in this tax year.
You will need to gross up the rent for these fees, as income and expenses should not be netted off. For example, if rent was £100, fees were £20 and you received £80 in the bank, you would show £100 of income with £20 management fees as an expense. The rental profit you have in the end will be the same.

Note that legal fees associated with the purchase or sale of a property are not allowable. These are deemed to be capital in nature and are used to reduce the chargeable capital gain when you sell the property.
Likewise, other legal fees will need to be reviewed to consider whether they relate to maintaining the value of the asset or concern the income you earn from it. For example, if you were subletting a property which you leased from someone else, legal fees relating to renegotiating the lease would be capital. Examples of allowable legal and professional fees would be: accountants and bookkeeper's fees, or legal fees associated with recovering rent from a tenant who had left without paying.

Boxes 32 and 35 Annual Investment Allowance and other capital allowances:
These are not available for residential properties, only commercial lets. Capital allowances for furnished holiday lets are entered on the previous page.

If you have a residential property rental and incur costs relating to upgrade or improvement of the property, for example adding an extension, these costs would be allowable in the capital gains tax computation when you sell it.

Box 37 – Rent a room relief:

This is rent received for renting a room in the home you live in. You can receive up to £7,500 (or £3,750 if let jointly) and report it as rent a room relief. Renting a room in your house with rental income up to this amount is received as tax free income. If you charge more than this in rent, you have the choice between paying tax on the amount over the limit or being taxed on your rental profit after deduction of expenses. The former option will be simpler to calculate, the latter may result in less tax to pay if your expenses are higher. If you choose to pay tax on the excess over the rent a room relief limit, you enter the amount of the relief in this box (£7,500 or £3,750).

Box 41, 42 & 43 – Losses:

Most rental property losses can only be set against future rental profits. There are exceptions where agricultural land is involved, but generally this is the case.

Therefore, any net loss on your rental property portfolio will probably be carried forward in **Box 43**.

55

Employment income – form SA102:

If you only have income under PAYE you do not have to complete a tax return. However, you if you do have other income which has to be reported, it will be necessary to enter income from your employment in this section in order to calculate your tax liability correctly.

If you hold an office and only receive reimbursed out of pocket expenses, you do not need to complete an employment page. HMRC advise that you write in the 'Any other information box' (**Box 19** on page TR7 of the main return) to say why you are not completing one.

Likewise, if you are a director but received no payments or benefits from your company, you can put in **Box 19** why you are not completing an employment page for that directorship.
Being a company director is a form of employment, even if you own your own company, so any salary paid to yourself by the company should be reported under this section.

HMRC regards that all company directors should file a tax return. However, it can be argued that the law says that this is only necessary if there is other taxable income to report or if HMRC request that you file a return. If you fall into this category, it will be your responsibility to consider whether this is necessary.

Examples of what is to be included in the employment income section are: salaries, wages, fees, commissions, overtime, bonuses, tips, lump sum payments, sick pay, maternity or paternity pay, and loans written off which were made because of your employment.

HMRC advises that any lump sum payments or interests in shares received should be explained on the additional information page on the tax return.

57

Page E1 & E2:

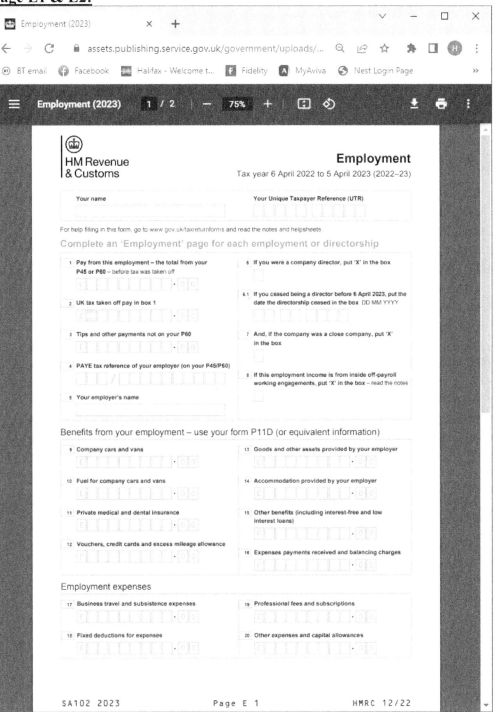

Employment

Tax year 6 April 2022 to 5 April 2023 (2022–23)

HM Revenue & Customs

Your name

Your Unique Taxpayer Reference (UTR)

For help filling in this form, go to www.gov.uk/taxreturnforms and read the notes and helpsheets.

Complete an 'Employment' page for each employment or directorship

1 Pay from this employment – the total from your P45 or P60 – before tax was taken off

2 UK tax taken off pay in box 1

3 Tips and other payments not on your P60

4 PAYE tax reference of your employer (on your P45/P60)

5 Your employer's name

6 If you were a company director, put 'X' in the box

6.1 If you ceased being a director before 6 April 2023, put the date the directorship ceased in the box DD MM YYYY

7 And, if the company was a close company, put 'X' in the box

8 If this employment income is from inside off-payroll working engagements, put 'X' in the box – read the notes

Benefits from your employment – use your form P11D (or equivalent information)

9 Company cars and vans

10 Fuel for company cars and vans

11 Private medical and dental insurance

12 Vouchers, credit cards and excess mileage allowance

13 Goods and other assets provided by your employer

14 Accommodation provided by your employer

15 Other benefits (including interest-free and low interest loans)

16 Expenses payments received and balancing charges

Employment expenses

17 Business travel and subsistence expenses

18 Fixed deductions for expenses

19 Professional fees and subscriptions

20 Other expenses and capital allowances

SA102 2023   Page E 1   HMRC 12/22

Pages E1 and E2 are essentially identical, giving you the opportunity to record more than one employment. This may be required if you were employed in more than one position at the same time, perhaps while working part-time, or if you have had more than one employer in the tax year.

If you have left a job, you can take information from your P45 to complete an employment page. You can then complete a second employment page using your P60, which your current employer should supply you at the end of the tax year.

Additional pages can be attached to the paper return as necessary.

'Complete an employment page for each employment or directorship':
The first section will be taken from your P45 or P60. The main things you will need to record will be your gross income in the tax year, PAYE deducted and the name and PAYE reference of your employer, all of which should appear on the P60 /P45.

Here you also state if you were a company director and if the company you worked for was a close company.

Close companies:
A close company is one that is controlled by five or fewer participators or any number of participators if they are all directors.

That generally means the sort of company that acts an alternative trading vehicle for an individual working on their own account or a small number of such persons.

Benefits from your employment:
In the next section you record taxable benefits you received from your employer in addition to your wages.

If you have anything to add to this section, your employer should have completed form P11D as part of their payroll process. They can give you a copy of this form in order to complete your tax return.

If a benefit is taxable, your employer pays Class 1A National Insurance and the amount of the benefit counts as part of your taxable income.

There is now an option to payroll some benefits, meaning that the tax due can be deducted from your salary throughout the year, instead of having to complete a tax return to correct the tax due. Benefits which can be dealt with in this way include car benefit, fuel benefit, private medical insurance and subscriptions such as gym membership.

Looking at page E1 of the form you will see some examples of benefits that are taxable. These include:

Box 12: Vouchers, credit cards and excess mileage allowance:
This category covers where you receive something which is not cash, but has an equivalent value to cash.

Credit card expenditure would fall into two categories: private use is a benefit; business use is not, although it used to be reportable on the P11D.

Box 13: Goods and other assets provided by your employer:
If your employer allows you use of a business asset for your private purposes.

Box 14: Accommodation provided by your employer:
This would cover the situation where you live in residential property owned by your employer and you pay a rent less than the market rate.

Boxes 9 & 10: Company cars and vans:
If there is any private use of a business vehicle, a car benefit results. The value of this benefit is calculated from the list price of the car and its CO_2 emissions level.
This does not apply if you have access to a pool car, but do not make any private use of it. Private use of a car would include commuting to work, but for a van ordinary commuting is exempt.

There may be other exceptions for insignificant private use for vans, for example if you use a van once a year to take some domestic waste to the tip. The example given by HMRC is a slight detour to buy a newspaper on the way to work. There is also no benefit if a van is only used for work trips or to travel between temporary workplaces.

The car benefit can be reduced by an employee contribution of up to £5,000. Up to this amount, the contribution reduces the taxable value of the car by the amount contributed.

If you make use of a company car and the company pays for fuel, where there is private use there will also be a fuel benefit. If the employee pays a contribution toward this, the benefit is only mitigated if the employee pays for all of the fuel.

Although most of the other benefits speak for themselves, one worth highlighting is:

Box 15 Other benefits (including interest-free and low interest loans):
A loan to an employee does not constitute a benefit if interest is charged at the commercial rate, which can be taken to mean the HMRC official interest rate. At the time of writing this was 2.00%; you can look up the interest rate for different tax years on the gov.uk website.

One specific example of an interest free loan is where a director has an overdrawn director's loan account.
This occurs where a director has drawn money out of the company in excess of the amount that they have been able to repay or to clear with dividends. This results because they do not wish to pay dividends or because there are insufficient profits in the company to do so.
An overdrawn director's loan account has two consequences. Firstly, if it is not repaid within nine months of the company's accounting year end, either by funds introduced by the director or by declaring dividends which are credited to the loan account, then the company must pay S455 tax on the balance at 33.75%. S455 tax is a special form of tax that can be reclaimed when the loan owed to the company is repaid.
The second consequence is that if the loan exceeds £10,000 at any point in the tax year then there is a taxable benefit which must be reported on form P11D and Class 1A National Insurance must be paid on the amount. The only way around this is for the company to charge interest on the loan at the official rate. This interest is then taxable for corporation tax.

If there is a benefit from an overdrawn loan account, the value of the loan multiplied by the official rate is entered in **Box 15**.

Payments on behalf of an employee:
This would include the situation if your employer paid a private utility bill on your behalf.
There are complicated tax rules concerning this area. Different arrangements, which you would think had the same end result, have different tax consequences. For example, if your employer were to pay your telephone bill for you, there would be different tax consequences according to whether they paid it direct, you paid it and claimed the money back from them or they gave you some extra money to pay it yourself!
If you are considering such an arrangement, you may find it less complicated to make a claim for business expenses instead.

Box 11 - Private medical insurance:
If your employer pays for this and you or a close relative benefit from it, then it must be reported here.

Employment expenses:
Generally, employees cannot claim expenses, unlike the self-employed, however there are some exceptions:
One example is where an employee uses a private car for business trips. Here they can claim tax relief at 45p per mile for the first 10,000 miles in a tax year and 25p per mile thereafter. There are also rates for motorbikes at 24p per mile, and bikes at 20p per mile, although these are not often used in practice.
You cannot claim for mileage on ordinary commuting between home and a permanent workplace. You can only claim for travelling between one place of work and another in the same employment or travelling between your home and a temporary workplace. A temporary workplace means somewhere you will work for less than two years.
Your employer can also reimburse you for business mileage at up to the above rates tax free. If they reimburse you at a lower rate, you can claim the difference as a relief on your tax return.

There are some professions who can claim for professional membership fees. You will be able to find a list of the ones approved by HMRC on the .gov.uk website.

In addition, there are some professionals who can claim a fixed deduction against their annual tax liability. For example, these would include fire fighters and nurses, who might receive a deduction to allow for the cost of cleaning their uniforms. Examples of the actual figures are: £125 for nurses, £140 for police officers and £140 for joiners and carpenters.

No benefit will arise if you incur expenses and your employer merely refunds them.

Employees can also claim a £6 per week use of home as office allowance, if working from home. This is a standard amount set by HMRC, which can be claimed without any additional admin.
If you are a self-employed person or a company director, you may be able to claim a greater amount than this, if you are prepared to keep the paperwork showing documentary evidence of the amount of extra expenses incurred, over and above what your utility and telephone bills would be if you were not working from home. You should also be prepared to supply HMRC with details of how you calculated the figure. You cannot include the cost of Council Tax in your calculation.

Self-employment form (Short) SA103S:

This is the most common reason for completing a tax return. The short self-employment return is for smaller businesses past their first year of trading. I will explain the conditions for using this form below. The full self-assessment form will be covered in the section following this one.

In order to use the short self-employment pages, your turnover for the year must be less than the VAT threshold (currently £85,000).

Secondly, it is permissible when summarising your income and expenses to use a year-end different to 5 April. If you have changed the date to which you prepare these figures in the year, you may not use the short self-assessment pages.

Finally, if the period over which you are taxed is different to your period of accounts you may not use the short self-assessment pages. This happens in the first two years of trading, where your accounting year end will be different to 5 April. I will explain the opening years' rules by which the taxable period is calculated in a later section.

The taxation of unincorporated businesses will move from a 'current year' basis to a 'tax year' basis from 2024/2025, with 2023/2024 being a year of transition to the new rules. This means that in future sole traders and partnerships will be taxed on their income within the tax year rather than within their accounting year as currently happens. There would then be less value in having an accounting year different to the tax year. In theory it might be possible within the new rules, but it would still be necessary to put together figures for the remainder of the tax year for the tax return.

65

Page SES 1:

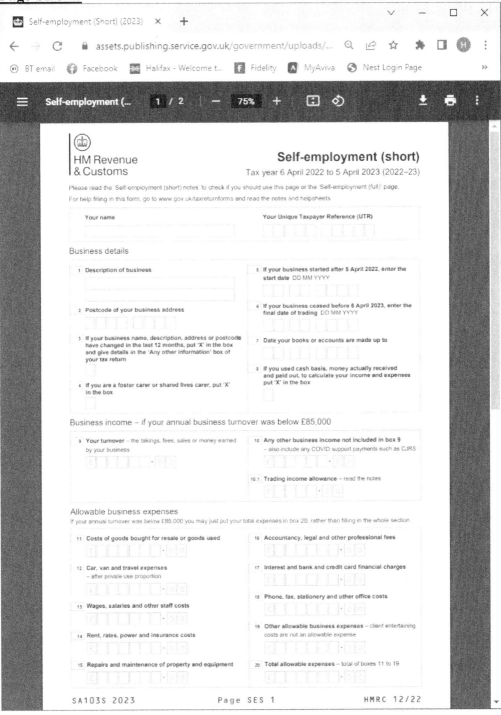

As with the other supplemental pages, the first two boxes identify you to HMRC as a specific individual taxpayer.

Business details:
Box 5 -7:
If your business has ceased in the tax year and you have no other taxable income, HMRC may remove you from self-assessment, after you have filed this year's tax return. However, you should not assume this will be the case. If you receive a request to file a tax return next year even though you have ceased, you may be able to get in contact with them to explain you no longer have any income except that which is taxed at source. In this circumstance, they may be able to remove you from self-assessment and therefore the need to file a tax return.

Your business may have an accounting period which is different from the tax year. This can be done for commercial reasons, for example so you can do your accounts at a time of year when your business is quiet, or for cash flow related purposes - for example a tax year end of 30 April will delay paying tax on those profits for almost a year (As I have said above this will cease to be an option from the 2024/2025 tax year onward).
One consequence of having a year-end different to the tax year can be that overlap profits result in the first 2-3 years of trading. Because of the opening year rules, a self-employed person with a non 5 April year end will be taxed twice on some of their profits in their first years. This amount is carried forward as overlap relief and is allowed as a deduction when you cease trading. Overlap profits are also affected if you change your accounting year end.

Business income:

Box 9: is for the total income from your main line of business. You will see that this section is for businesses with gross turnover of less than £85,000. As a side note I would note that if your income is over this you should be registering for VAT.

This income will include all payments for services or goods sold, and any payments in kind. By a payment in kind, I mean where you receive a service or goods instead of money, in exchange for whatever you sell or whatever service you provide.

The income recorded in this box should also include the value of work carried out in the year for which you have not yet been paid.

Box 10: is for other business income which might be generated incidental to your main line of business, e.g. if you operated a service collecting building waste, you might have a sideline selling scrap metal.
Other examples given by HMRC would be rental income from the letting of surplus business property which became temporarily available or payments for a right to cross your land (known as 'Wayleaves').

Allowable business expenses:

These will include (but are not limited to) purchases of stock, wages, rent, lighting, postage, stationery, telephone costs and the business proportion of fuel and motor insurance.

If you work from home, you can only claim the business proportion of your household costs. There are two systems to keep track of the business proportion. Firstly, you can keep detailed records that demonstrate the actual cost to the business, for example keeping copies of phone bills showing the cost of business calls.
It is more common however, to use a second system, where you bring into your accounts a standard £6 per week. This is an amount approved by HMRC for use of home as office.

Box 11: is for your purchases, which would be products that you sell or items directly used in the making of the product or service you provide.

Box 12: requires an adjustment for private use of a business vehicle or a private proportion of fuel. This would include commuting to work from your home; however, if you are an itinerant trader such as a builder, fuel costs to customers' sites where you do work are allowable.

Entertainment:

Note that the form says that client entertaining is not an allowable expense. There are various rules relating to entertaining and gifts. A brief summary of the main points would be as follows:

1. The cost of annual parties for employees is allowable, but should be restricted to £150 per head to avoid any P11D benefit resulting.

2. The cost of trivial benefits such as Christmas gifts for employees is allowable, but only where individual gifts do not exceed £50. For a company director the total benefits cannot exceed £300 in a tax year.

3. Gifts for clients are generally not allowable, unless they carry conspicuous advertising – for example pens or t-shirts with the business name on. Again, there is a limit to the value allowable of £50.

4. Gifts of food, alcohol and tobacco are never allowable.

5. Client entertaining is not allowable for tax purposes. It is common to show this as an entry on a set of accounts, which is then added back before calculating tax due.

One tax tip arising from point 2 above for director shareholders is that you could buy yourself £50 in vouchers six times a year and so extract £300 from the company which would be corporation tax deductible. You must make sure that the vouchers are not exchangeable for cash otherwise a P11D benefit could result.

Self-employment (Short) (2023)   ×   +

← → C   🔒 assets.publishing.service.gov.uk/government/uploads/...   ⊕ 🔖 ☆   🔖 ◻ 🅗 ⋮

🖂 BT email   Facebook   Halifax - Welcome t...   Fidelity   MyAviva   Nest Login Page   »

☰   Self-employment (...   2 / 2   —   75%   +   ⊡ ◇   ⬇ 🖶 ⋮

Net profit or loss

21 **Net profit** – if your business income is more than your expenses (if box 9 + box 10 minus box 20 is positive)

22 **Or, net loss** – if your expenses exceed your business income (if box 20 minus (box 9 + box 10) is positive)

Tax allowances for certain buildings, vehicles and equipment (capital allowances)
Do not include the cost of these in your business expenses.

23 Annual Investment Allowance

25.1 The Structures and Buildings Allowance

24 Allowance for small balance of unrelieved expenditure

25.2 Freeport Structures and Buildings Allowance

24.1 Zero-emission car allowance

26 Total balancing charges – for example, where you have disposed of items for more than their tax value

25 Other capital allowances

Calculating your taxable profits
Your taxable profit may not be the same as your net profit. Please read the 'Self-employment (short) notes' to see if you need to make any adjustments and fill in the boxes which apply to arrive at your taxable profit for the year.

27 Goods and/or services for your own use

28 Net business profit for tax purposes (if box 21 + box 26 + box 27 minus (boxes 22 to 25.2) is positive). Or if you've completed box 10.1 (box 21 + box 26 + box 27 minus box 10.1)

29 Loss brought forward from earlier years set off against this year's profits – up to the amount in box 28

30 Any other business income not included in box 9 or box 10

Total taxable profits or net business loss
If your total profits from all Self-employments and Partnerships for 2022–23 are less than £6,725, you do not have to pay Class 2 National Insurance contributions, but you may want to pay voluntarily (box 36) to protect your rights to certain benefits.

31 Total taxable profits from this business (if box 28 + box 30 minus box 29 is positive)

32 Net business loss for tax purposes (if boxes 22 to 25.2 minus (box 21 + box 26 + box 27) is positive)

Losses, Class 2 and Class 4 National Insurance contributions (NICs) and CIS deductions
If you've made a loss for tax purposes (box 32), read the 'Self-employment (short) notes' and fill in boxes 33 to 35 as appropriate.

33 Loss from this tax year set off against other income for 2022–23

34 Loss to be carried back to previous years and set off against income (or capital gains)

35 Total loss to carry forward after all other set-offs – including unused losses brought forward

36 If your total profits for 2022–23 are less than £6,725 and you choose to pay Class 2 NICs voluntarily, put 'X' in the box

37 If you're exempt from paying Class 4 NICs, put 'X' in the box

38 Total Construction Industry Scheme (CIS) deductions taken from your payments by contractors – CIS subcontractors only

SA103S 2023   Page SES 2

Net Profit or loss:
Boxes 21 and 22: are the result of netting off your income and expenses on the previous page. If expenses are higher than income, you fill in **Box 22** and if income is higher than expenses **Box 21**.

Tax allowances for certain buildings, vehicles and equipment (capital allowances):
Boxes 23 & 25: Tax allowances:
Capital allowances are a complicated area, which I will try to summarise briefly, but don't expect this to be too thorough.

In accounts production, it is common to depreciate the assets of a business to reflect the reduction in their working life. However, depreciation is not tax deductible, so it is added back in calculating a person or company's tax liability. In place of this, capital allowances are used to reflect the aging of assets for tax purposes.

If the purchase of an asset has a material cost, it will be capitalised. Examples of this would be a computer, office furniture, or a business vehicle. Smaller value items would instead be put to expenses in the accounts, so for example whereas a computer might be capitalised, replacement toner cartridges might be recorded as stationery expense.

Capital allowances are calculated based on the total value of assets capitalised. These come in two main forms:

Annual Investment Allowance allows you to deduct all of the cost of an asset in the year you purchase it, up to an annual limit for total expenditure. It is a kind of capital allowance which offers tax relief at 100% of qualifying expenditure in the year of purchase.

Anything that does not qualify for this or which is in excess of the annual limit is written down by 18% (or 6% for high emission motor cars). That means 18% of the value is deductible, the rest being carried forward to the next year, at which time 18% of the remaining balance is again deductible, and so on.

Most plant and machinery, including vans and trucks, but not cars, qualifies for Annual Investment Allowance.

Since 1st January 2019 the annual limit for Annual Investment Allowance has been £1,000,000.

For limited companies there is a 130% tax relief on purchases of plant and machinery called the capital allowance super deduction. This means assets purchased by limited companies up to 31 March 2023 can receive a deduction against taxable profits of up to 130% of their cost price.

Calculating your taxable profits:

Box 27: This is a deduction for stock that you used yourself instead of selling it. Own consumption is not tax deductible.

Box 29: This allows you to deduct losses from previous years of trading from the current year profits.

Loss relief rules:

Trade losses can be relieved against other income or possibly capital gains in the same year. In this case, normally the whole of the loss is claimed against the other income. Any remaining loss may then be used against chargeable gains.

Remaining losses can also be carried forward to set against future profits of the same trade. This is usually the default option if you do not state otherwise.

Note that you can offset a loss against the previous year's other income as well, which could result in you getting a refund on tax paid previously.

There are two special loss reliefs for businesses that have recently started or those that have ceased.

Early years loss relief allows losses in the first four years of trade to be carried back against the other income of the previous three years. The losses are carried back to the earliest year, then applied to the next year if any losses remain and so on.

Terminal loss relief is used when a business ceases. Losses in the final 12 months of trading can be carried back up to three years.

You must say that the claim is for terminal loss relief and provide details of the amount of the loss used for each year in the 'Any other information' box and enter the amount in **Box 34**.

Loss relief limit:

A maximum of £50,000 or 25% of adjusted total income for self-employed people can be relieved by losses each year.

> Note that there are different loss relief rules again for limited companies, which I will not cover here since I am not talking about how to complete corporation tax returns.

Losses, Class 2 and Class 4 NICS and CIS Deductions:

Boxes 36 & 37: Class 4 National Insurance:

If you are self-employed, unless your profits fall below a certain threshold, you will also be due to pay Class 2 and Class 4 National Insurance. Class 2 is a fixed amount per week and Class 4 is calculated on your profits in virtually the same way as your income tax. Both are payable at the same time as any income tax liability.

Box 37 refers to the circumstance where your profits are below the threshold for Class 4 and you have applied for an exemption to paying it.

Annual Profits	Class 2 NI due	Class 4 NI due
Below £6,725	0	0
£6,725-£11,907	£3.15 / week	0
£11,908-£50,270	£3.15 / week	9.73% of profits
More than £50,270	£3.15 / week	2.73% of profits above this level

Box 38: Construction Industry Scheme:

If you work in the trades and have been self-employed as a subcontractor, CIS tax may have been deducted from the amount paid to you. This amount should be included in **Box 38**. As this is tax already paid, it is deducted from your final tax liability. If you have paid more CIS than the tax that is due, you will be due a refund.

Self-Employment (full) SA103F:

If your turnover was £85,000 or more, or you have changed your accounting year end date, you must use the full self-employment form. Likewise, you must do so if your basis period is not the same as your accounting year end. This will occur in the first two years of trading if your accounting year end is not the same as the tax year.

75

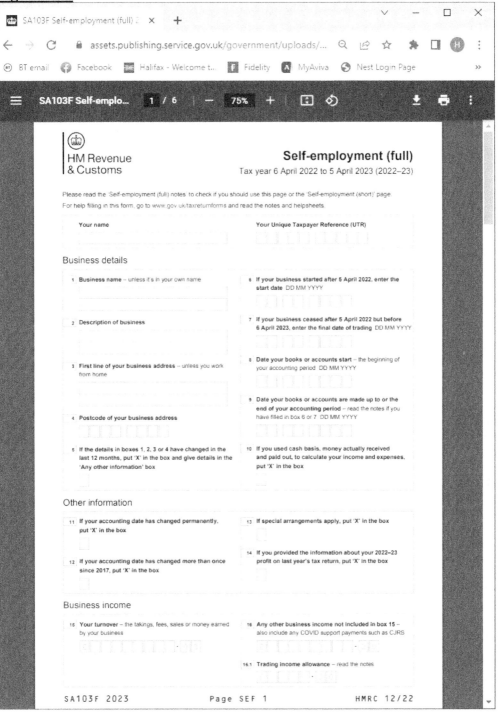

There is a little bit more information required here than on the first page of the short self-assessment return, but you will see it is essentially the same page.

Page SEF 2:

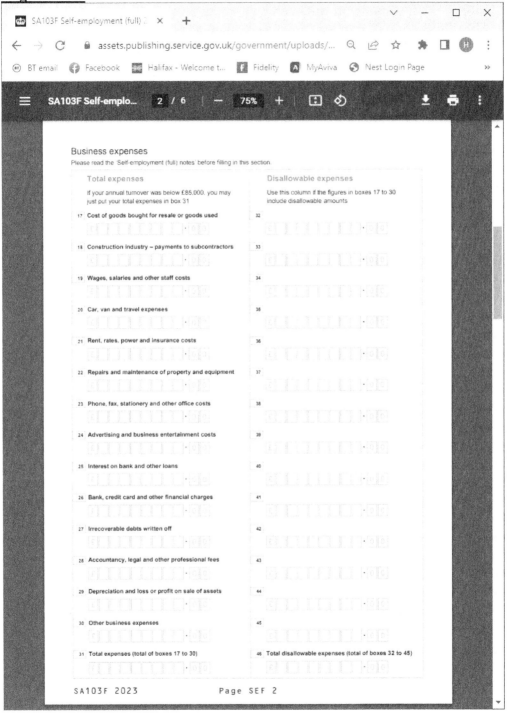

Business expenses

Please read the 'Self-employment (full) notes' before filling in this section.

Total expenses	Disallowable expenses
If your annual turnover was below £85,000, you may just put your total expenses in box 31	Use this column if the figures in boxes 17 to 30 include disallowable amounts

17 Cost of goods bought for resale or goods used
£ · 0 0

32
£ · 0

18 Construction industry – payments to subcontractors
£ · 0 0

33
£ · 0

19 Wages, salaries and other staff costs
£ · 0 0

34
£ · 0

20 Car, van and travel expenses
£ · 0 0

35
£ · 0

21 Rent, rates, power and insurance costs
£ · 0 0

36
£ · 0

22 Repairs and maintenance of property and equipment
£ · 0 0

37
£ · 0

23 Phone, fax, stationery and other office costs
£ · 0 0

38
£ · 0

24 Advertising and business entertainment costs
£ · 0 0

39
£ · 0

25 Interest on bank and other loans
£ · 0 0

40
£ · 0

26 Bank, credit card and other financial charges
£ · 0 0

41
£ · 0

27 Irrecoverable debts written off
£ · 0 0

42
£ · 0

28 Accountancy, legal and other professional fees
£ · 0 0

43
£ · 0

29 Depreciation and loss or profit on sale of assets
£ · 0 0

44
£ · 0

30 Other business expenses
£ · 0 0

45
£ · 0

31 Total expenses (total of boxes 17 to 30)
£ · 0 0

46 Total disallowable expenses (total of boxes 32 to 45)
£ · 0

78

You will see from the previous page that on the full self-assessment form the business expenses section has been expanded.

Before filling this in you will need to prepare a simple set of accounts or a trial balance. This means listing your income, expenses, assets and liabilities such that the expenses and assets add up to an equal and opposite value to the income and liabilities. There will be a balancing figure for your profit or loss from previous years, if this is not your first year of trading.

Once again, there are whole books written on preparing accounts, so I won't go much further than that and will continue to assume your business is simple enough that you can put together such a trial balance for yourself. There is a simple example of how to prepare accounts from a trial balance in one of the appendices to this book.

You are not required to draw up a full set of formal accounts, but you must keep sufficient records to support the information that you supply to HMRC. You should keep business records for at least seven years in case HMRC request more information on one of your tax returns.

Example trial balance:		
Description	Debit £	Credit £
Sales		10,000
Purchases	4,000	
Stationery	300	
Rent	1,000	
Computer equipment	2,000	
Debtors	500	
Creditors		500
Profit / retained profit	2,700	
TOTAL	10,500	10,500

Sales down to Rent are the income and expenses, Computer equipment and Debtors are assets and Creditors is a liability.

Of course, if you were preparing accounts for someone else to look at, it would be common to depreciate an asset such as computer equipment. Depreciation is designed to reflect how an asset is used up over its lifetime. It is an example of something which is commonly put into accounts to make them more representative of an actual business situation, but which is not allowable for tax purposes.
This is what the second column of Page SES 2 concerns ('Disallowable Expenses'). If you have included figures for accounting purposes which are not allowable for tax, you put the disallowable amount in the second column.
Other examples would be profit or loss on sale of an asset, fines or penalties for late filing of VAT returns, costs of entertaining customers or a private element of an expense.

If you are filing in this form, you may be VAT registered. If you are using the traditional accounting basis for VAT, your income and deductions would typically exclude VAT. If you are using the cash basis, your income and expenses would typically include VAT.

If you choose to include VAT when completing your return, you either put your net VAT payment to HMRC as an expense in **Box 30** or a net VAT repayment received from HMRC in **Box 16**.
You should not include recoverable VAT when working out capital allowances on plant & machinery that you purchased in the year.

Box 25: Interest on bank and other loans:
Note that if you have a business loan, you would include here the interest charged on the loan in the tax year, not the business repayments.

Page SEF 3:

Net profit or loss

47 Net profit – if your business income is more than your expenses (if box 15 + box 16 minus box 31 is positive)

48 Or, net loss – if your expenses are more than your business income (if box 31 minus (box 15 + box 16) is positive)

Tax allowances for vehicles and equipment (capital allowances)

There are 'capital' tax allowances for vehicles, equipment and certain buildings used in your business (do not include the cost of these in your business expenses). Please read the 'Self-employment (full) notes' and use the examples to work out your capital allowances.

49 Annual Investment Allowance

50 Capital allowances at 18% on equipment, including cars with lower CO2 emissions

51 Capital allowances at 6% on equipment, including cars with higher CO2 emissions

52 Zero-emission goods vehicle allowance

52.1 Zero-emission car allowance

53 The Structures and Buildings Allowance

53.1 Freeport Structures and Buildings Allowance

54 Electric charge-point allowance

55 100% and other enhanced capital allowances

56 Allowances on sale or cessation of business use (where you've disposed of assets for less than their tax value)

57 Total capital allowances (total of boxes 49 to 56)

Box 58 is not in use

59 Balancing charge on sales of assets or on the cessation of business use (including where Business Premises Renovation Allowance has been claimed) for example, where you've disposed of assets for more than their tax value

Calculating your taxable profit or loss

You may have to adjust your net profit or loss for disallowable expenses or capital allowances to arrive at your taxable profit or your loss for tax purposes. Please read the 'Self-employment (full) notes' and fill in the boxes below that apply.

60 Goods and services for your own use

61 Total additions to net profit or deductions from net loss (box 46 + box 59 + box 60)

62 Income, receipts and other profits included in business income or expenses but not taxable as business profits

63 Total deductions from net profit or additions to net loss (box 57 + box 62)

64 Net business profit for tax purposes (if box 47 + box 61 minus (box 48 + box 63) is positive)

65 Net business loss for tax purposes (if box 48 + box 63 minus (box 47 + box 61) is positive)

With a bit of expansion, this page is a lot like the second page of the short self-assessment return.

Tax allowances:

For most asset purchases Annual Investment Allowance is available, except for land & property and cars. So the total expenditure on plant & machinery, fixtures, computer equipment, trucks and vans can be entered in **Box 49**, up to the level of the annual allowance.

Expenditure over this amount on those items goes into the general pool for capital allowances and is then written down each year.

Cars are allocated to the general or special rate pools according to their level of CO_2 emissions. Anything over 50g/km is currently allocated to the special rate pool.

The value of the general pool x 18% is written down each year.

The value of the special rate pool x 6% is written down each year.

The written down amount is claimed against taxable income and the balance carried forward to future years.

The amount of writing down allowances written down from the general pool is entered in **Box 50**.

The amount of writing down allowances written down from the special rate pool is entered in **Box 51**.

If you sell an asset there may be a balancing charge or allowance to bring in. This is calculated as the proceeds of the sale, including part exchange value, less the written down value of the asset. Where Annual Investment Allowance has been claimed, the written down value will be zero.

If the proceeds are less than the written down value or zero, there will be a balancing allowance equal to the amount by which the written down value exceeds the proceeds.

If the proceeds are greater than written down value, there will be a balancing charge equal to the difference.

A balancing allowance is entered in **Box 56**. A balancing charge is entered in **Box 59**.

The small pools allowance is for the situation where the value of the general or special rate pool is £1,000 of less. In this case you can write down the value of the whole pool in the current year. The value of the small pools allowance goes in **Box 50 or 51**, according to whether you are writing off the balance on the general or special rate pools.

Page SEF 4:

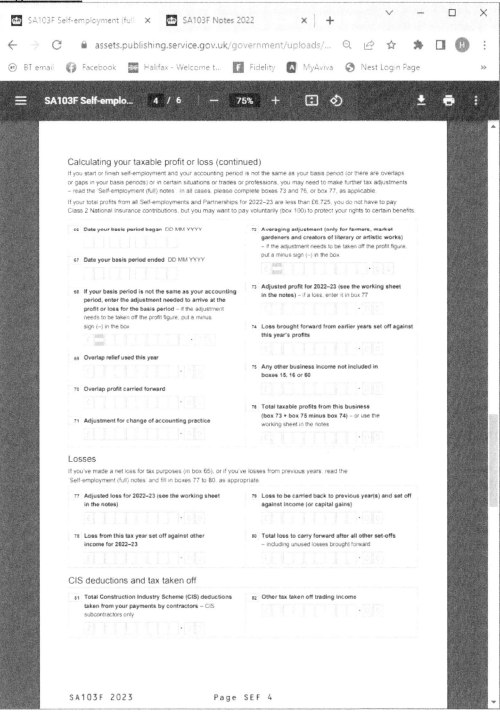

Calculating your taxable profit or loss (continued)

If you start or finish self-employment and your accounting period is not the same as your basis period (or there are overlaps or gaps in your basis periods) or in certain situations or trades or professions, you may need to make further tax adjustments – read the 'Self-employment (full) notes'. In all cases, please complete boxes 73 and 76, or box 77, as applicable.

If your total profits from all Self-employments and Partnerships for 2022–23 are less than £6,725, you do not have to pay Class 2 National Insurance contributions, but you may want to pay voluntarily (box 100) to protect your rights to certain benefits.

66 Date your basis period began DD MM YYYY

67 Date your basis period ended DD MM YYYY

68 If your basis period is not the same as your accounting period, enter the adjustment needed to arrive at the profit or loss for the basis period – if the adjustment needs to be taken off the profit figure, put a minus sign (–) in the box

69 Overlap relief used this year

70 Overlap profit carried forward

71 Adjustment for change of accounting practice

72 Averaging adjustment (only for farmers, market gardeners and creators of literary or artistic works) – if the adjustment needs to be taken off the profit figure, put a minus sign (–) in the box

73 Adjusted profit for 2022–23 (see the working sheet in the notes) – if a loss, enter it in box 77

74 Loss brought forward from earlier years set off against this year's profits

75 Any other business income not included in boxes 15, 16 or 60

76 Total taxable profits from this business (box 73 + box 75 minus box 74) – or use the working sheet in the notes

Losses

If you've made a net loss for tax purposes (in box 65), or if you've losses from previous years, read the 'Self-employment (full) notes' and fill in boxes 77 to 80, as appropriate.

77 Adjusted loss for 2022–23 (see the working sheet in the notes)

78 Loss from this tax year set off against other income for 2022–23

79 Loss to be carried back to previous year(s) and set off against income (or capital gains)

80 Total loss to carry forward after all other set-offs – including unused losses brought forward

CIS deductions and tax taken off

81 Total Construction Industry Scheme (CIS) deductions taken from your payments by contractors – CIS subcontractors only

82 Other tax taken off trading income

84

This page follows on from the calculation of your taxable profit or loss on the previous page.

Opening years rules:

One of the conditions for having to complete the full self-employed section is if your taxable period is different to the period of the accounts you have prepared.

This happens if you change your accounting year end and also in the first two years of trading where your accounting year end is not equal to the tax year.

The first year of trade you will be taxed on the period from commencement to 5 April.

The second year you will be taxed according to the following rules:

If your accounts year falls in the year to 5 April and it is more than 12 months after the date your business began, you will be taxed on the 12 months *to that* accounting date.

If your accounts year falls in the year to 5 April and it is less than 12 months after you started in business, you will be taxed on the 12 months *from* the date you started.

If you do not have an accounting date in the year to 5 April, you will be taxed on the 12 months to 5 April.

The third year you are taxed on your accounting year.

Because the opening year rules result in income being taxed more than once, overlap profits result, which can be relieved when you change your accounting year or cease to trade.

In the 2024/25 the basis period of taxation will be changing from an accounting year basis to a taxation year basis, with 2023/24 being a transitional year. This means that businesses that prepare accounts to a year end different to 5th April or 31st March will have to pro-rate their results to the tax year.

Boxes 69 & 70: If you have changed your accounting year or ceased, you will enter the calculated overlap relief in **Box 69**. Otherwise overlap relief that still exists will be carried forward in **Box 70**.

As explained in the box above, the overlap relief is the profit that has been taxed twice because of the way the opening years rules work.

You should keep a record of the overlap profit taxed twice and the overlap period (number of days taxed twice).

Boxes 74 & 77-80: You will see there is a box for losses in the main section and then a separate box for losses as well.

Loss Relief:

One option for relieving a loss is to carry it forward for use against future profits in the same trade. A loss brought forward can only be used in this way.

If you have any such losses from a previous year, you can enter the amount in **Box 74**, which will then be set against current year profits.

Getting on to the main section of losses:

After tax adjustments, if you have made a loss rather than a profit, you would enter it in **Box 77** instead of **Box 73**.

A loss in the current year can also be used against profits from other income (for example bank interest or employment income) in the current or previous year. To set a loss off against current year profits put the amount to offset in **Box 78**, or use **Box 79** to set the losses against other income in a previous year.

Note that you can set losses against the current or prior year in the order of your choosing, however the profits of the year you are reducing must be completely eliminated before offsetting any losses against the other year. Any remaining loss to carry forward is then entered in **Box 80**.

There is a limit on the amount of profits that can be relieved by losses. This limit is the greater of £50,000 or 25% of an individual's adjusted total income.

Box 81: is for any Construction Industry Scheme deductions made by a business for which you have acted as a subcontractor. As these should already have been paid over by that business to HMRC, the amount entered here will reduce your tax liability and sometimes result in a refund if your tax liability is less than the deductions taken.

87

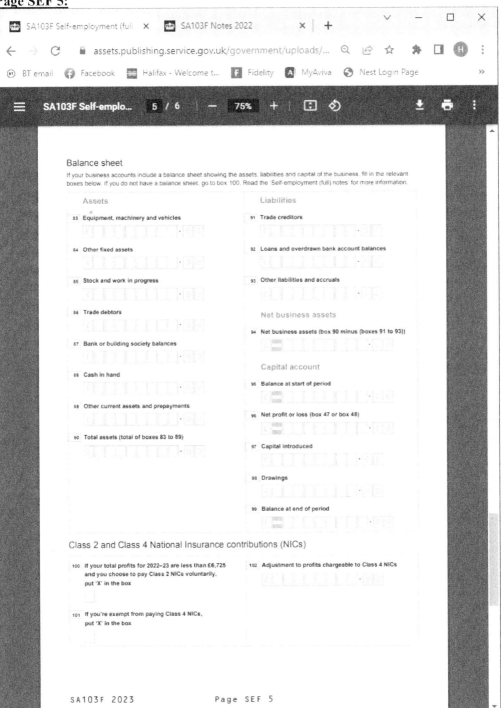

This page is mostly about the balance sheet.
In short total assets – total liabilities = the capital account balance.

The capital account is made up of the opening balance, plus the profit or loss taken from page SEF 3. It is also adjusted for money that you have introduced into the business and drawings you have taken out of it.
An example of capital introduced would be if you took out a personal loan to invest in the business and paid the money received into your business bank account.
Drawings are any personal expenses paid through the business account and any lump sum amounts withdrawn which you may feel represent your wages. An owner's wages are treated differently from those of employees, who will be paid through PAYE. Amounts taken by the proprietor of a business are classified as drawings instead (although if instead you are a company director, you can pay yourself a salary through the payroll, as a company is a separate legal entity from the director who runs it).

Your capital account might be overdrawn, i.e. have a debit balance. This happens when the total liabilities are greater than total assets. This is analogous to the director of a company having an overdrawn loan account, although it is less serious.
There is only really one penalty to having an overdrawn capital account, which is that HMRC may disallow some of your loan interest. If you have a loan and an overdrawn current account, it could be viewed by them that you are financing your private drawings with the loan. In this case, if accumulated depreciation in the accounts is less than the overdrawn balance, a proportion of the loan interest may be disallowed.

Page SEF 6:

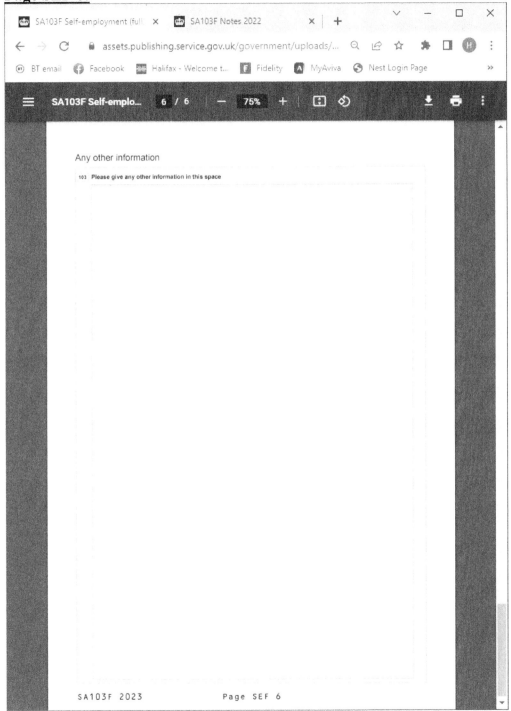

Any other information

103 Please give any other information in this space

90

This is space for any other information which you feel HMRC may require to understand the entries in the self-employment section of the tax return.

Partnership statement – form SA104:

If you earned self-employed income in a partnership, as well as your personal tax return you will additionally be required to complete a partnership tax return. This details the total income and expenses of the business, a little like self-employed income is recorded on form SA103. Although I will not be going into the partnership return in detail, there are some notes on it in the appendices of this book. After completing the partnership tax return, you will then need to enter your share of the partnership income on form SA104 within your personal tax return.

Note that just like the personal self-assessment tax return, the partnership tax return carries penalties for late filing.

Like the self-employment form, there is a full and a short partnership statement.
Most partnerships only need to complete the short partnership pages.
The short partnership statement is for those businesses that only have trading income and untaxed bank or building society interest. The full statement covers a wider range of types of income that might be received by a partnership.

93

Page SP01:

Partnership × Partnership × Partnership × +

assets.publishing.service.gov.uk/government...

BT email Facebook Halifax - Welcome t... Fidelity MyAviva Nest Login Page

Partnership (s... 1 / 2 75%

HM Revenue
& Customs

Partnership (short)

Tax year 6 April 2021 to 5 April 2022 (2021–22)

Your name

Your Unique Taxpayer Reference (UTR)

Complete a 'Partnership' page for each partnership of which you were a member and for each partnership business.
For help filling in this form, go to www.gov.uk/taxreturnforms and read the notes and helpsheets.

Partnership details

1 **Partnership reference number**

2 **Description of partnership trade or profession**

3 **If you became a partner after 5 April 2021, enter the date you joined the partnership** DD MM YYYY

4 **If you left the partnership after 5 April 2021 and before 6 April 2022, enter the date you left**

5 **If the partnership used cash basis, money actually received and paid out, to calculate its income and expenses, put 'X' in the box** – read the notes

Your share of the partnership's trading or professional profits

Please refer to the Partnership Statement to complete these pages and if you need any help, read the 'Partnership (short) notes'.
If you want to enter a loss, or an adjustment needs to be taken off, put a minus sign (–) in the box next to the £ sign.

6 **Date your basis period began** DD MM YYYY

7 **Date your basis period ended** DD MM YYYY

8 **Your share of the partnership's profit or loss** – from box 11 or box 12 on the Partnership Statement

£ .00

9 **If your basis period is not the same as the partnership's accounting period, enter the adjustment needed to arrive at the profit or loss for your basis period**

£ .00

9.1 **Self-Employment Income Support Scheme grant received in the year to 5 April 2022**

£ .00

10 **Adjustment for change of accounting practice** – from box 11A on the Partnership Statement

£ .00

11 **Averaging adjustment** – only for farmers, market gardeners and creators of literary or artistic works

£ .00

12 **Foreign tax claimed as a deduction** – only if Foreign Tax Credit Relief is not being claimed on the 'Foreign' pages

£ .00

13 **Overlap relief used this year**

£ .00

14 **Overlap profit carried forward**

£ .00

Box 15 is not in use

16 **Adjusted profit for 2021–22** – see the working sheet in the notes

£ .00

17 **Losses brought forward from earlier years set off against this year's profit (up to the amount in box 16)**

£ .00

18 **Taxable profits after losses brought forward (box 16 minus box 17)**

£ .00

19 **Any other business income not included in the partnership accounts**

£ .00

20 **Your share of total taxable profits from the partnership's business for 2021–22 (box 18 + box 19)**

£ .00

SA104S 2022 Page SP 1 HMRC 12/21

As per previous pages, the first boxes help HMRC identify which taxpayer the return relates to. In addition to your personal Unique Taxpayer Reference, the partnership itself will have a UTR. This number is entered in **Box 1**.

If you join a partnership within a tax year, you will be taxed on your share of the partnership profits to 5 April, following the rules for the opening years of self-employment.

If you leave a partnership within the tax year, you will only be taxed on your share of the profits from the start of the accounts year to the date you left. There will be an adjustment if any profits were taxed twice under the opening years rules (the overlap relief which I have described earlier in the self-employment sections).

Box 8 & 9:
You will enter your share of the profits from the partnership in **Box 8**. As with a sole trader, there will be a different basis period in the first two or three years of trading. The adjustment to get to the profit that is taxable is entered in **Box 9**.

For convenience, I have repeated my opening years box out below.

Opening years rules:
The first year of trade you will be taxed on the period from commencement to 5 April.

The second year you will be taxed according to the following rules:
If your accounts year falls in the year to 5 April and it is more than 12 months after the date your business began, you will be taxed on the 12 months *to that* accounting date.

If your accounts year falls in the year to 5 April and it is less than 12 months after you started in business, you will be taxed on the 12 months *from* the date you started.

If you do not have an accounting date in the year to 5 April, you will be taxed on the 12 months to 5 April.

The third year you are taxed on your accounting year.

In the 2024/25 the basis period of taxation will be changing from an accounting year basis to a taxation year basis, with 2023/24 being a transitional year. This means that businesses that prepare accounts to a year

---

end different to 5th April or 31st March will have to pro-rate their results to the tax year.

Your share of partnership's trading and professional profits:
The basis period referred to here is the accounting period of the partnership.

Your share of the partnership's profits will be taken from the partnership return, and will have been agreed with your partners when you started working with them. It may be that you are splitting profits equally or you may have a greater or lower profit share, for example if you participate to a greater or lesser degree in the venture than another partner.

Boxes 13, 14 & 17:
Because you will be taxed in your first year to 5 April regardless of the partnership's year end, overlap relief can result. This happens where the partnership's year end is different from 5 April. In this case, the opening years rules mean you may be taxed on some of your profits twice in the first years of trading. These profits are carried forward and are relieved when you cease trading. Overlap relief also changes if the partnership changes its year end.
If overlap relief is used (which it will if the year end changes) it is entered in **Box 13**.
If profits have been taxed twice in the initial years of your trading, you can record the amount of the overlap to be carried forward in **Box 14**.

Losses on previous year's partnership returns can be offset against profits in the current year. In order to make use of these losses, you record them in **Box 17**.

Boxes 3 and 4:
These enable you to enter the date of joining or leaving an existing partnership.

Page SP02:

Your share of the partnership's trading or professional losses

21 Adjusted loss for 2021–22 – see the working sheet in the notes

£ [   ] . [ ][ ]

23 Loss to be carried back to previous year(s) and set off against income (or capital gains)

£ [   ] . [ ][ ]

22 Loss from this tax year set off against other income for 2021–22

£ [   ] . [ ][ ]

24 Total loss to carry forward after all other set-offs – including unused losses brought forward

£ [   ] . [ ][ ]

Class 2 and Class 4 National Insurance contributions (NICs)

If your total profits from all self-employments and partnerships for 2021–22 are less than £6,515 you do not have to pay Class 2 NICs, but you may want to pay voluntarily (box 25) to protect your rights to certain benefits. Read the Partnership (short) notes.

25 If your total profits for 2021–22 are less than £6,515 and you choose to pay Class 2 NICs voluntarily, put 'X' in the box

[ ]

26 If you're exempt from paying Class 4 NICs, put 'X' in the box

[ ]

27 Adjustment to profits chargeable to Class 4 NICs

£ [   ] . [ ][ ]

Your share of the partnership's untaxed interest

28 Your share of untaxed interest – from box 13 on the Partnership Statement

£ [   ] . [ ][ ]

Your share of the partnership's tax paid and deductions

Box 29 is not in use

30 Your share of Construction Industry Scheme deductions made by contractors – from box 24 on the Partnership Statement

£ [   ] . [ ][ ]

31 Your share of any tax taken off trading income (not contractor deductions) – from box 24A on the Partnership Statement

£ [   ] . [ ][ ]

Any other information

32 Please give any other information in this space

[   ]

SA104S 2022   Page SP 2

98

Your share of the partnership's trading or professional losses:
The first section (**Boxes 21 – 24**) records losses in the current year, which will be used against profits from other income in the year, such as bank interest or employment income. Losses carried forward are also recorded here.

Note that you can offset a loss against the previous year's other income as well, which could result in you getting a refund on tax paid previously. A loss can also be carried back to offset a profit in the previous year from the same trade.

I have elsewhere already mentioned about other loss reliefs available, such as early years relief or terminal loss relief.

There is a limit on the amount of profits that can be relieved by losses. This limit is the greater of £50,000 or 25% of an individual's adjusted total income.

Class 4 National Insurance contributions (NICs):
If you are self-employed, unless your profits fall below a certain threshold, you will also be due to pay Class 2 and Class 4 National Insurance. Class 2 is a fixed amount and Class 4 is calculated on your profits in virtually the same as income tax. Both are payable at the same time as any income tax liability. See the self-employment section earlier, where I produced a table showing the thresholds for these taxes.

Note that you do not have to pay Class 4 if you reach state pension age before the beginning of the tax year.

Your share of the partnership untaxed interest etc:
Box 28:
It is usual practice when calculating the taxable profits of a partnership to take out interest received. Each partner's share of the interest received in the tax year to 5 April is then brought into their personal tax return. Note that the interest recorded on the personal tax return is based on the amount received in the tax year, which may be different from the amount received in the partnership accounts if your partnership has an accounts year different to the tax year.

You will enter in **Box 28** your share of any bank or building society interest.

Box 30: Construction Industry Scheme deductions:

If you work in the trades and have been self-employed as a subcontractor, CIS tax may have been deducted from the amount paid to you. Your share of the deductions on any partnership income is included in **Box 30**. As this is tax already paid, it is deducted from your final tax liability. If you have paid more CIS than the tax that is due, you will be due a refund.

Appendix 1 – Professional accounting bodies:

If you have come to the point where you feel you need the services of a professional accountant, you may find it useful to know what the many qualifications and professional bodies mean.

These are the main ones:

Association of Chartered Certified Accountants

This is one of the two main professional bodies. They will be well qualified to prepare a set of accounts and to deal with your day-to-day tax affairs. The ACCA has global recognition and extends its reach into other areas of accounting, such as management accountancy.

Institute of Chartered Accountants in England and Wales

This is the second of the two main professional bodies. Again, they will be able to very competently prepare accounts and tax returns. They are also focussed on auditing, which is where bigger businesses need aspects of their accounts independently verified.

As the audit threshold for turnover and net assets is in the low millions, I have assumed this is not one of your requirements!

Chartered Tax Adviser

These accountants specialise in tax law, but will also be able to prepare accounts for you.

Others: **AAT and ATT**:

These letters stand for the Association of Accounting Technicians and the Association of Taxation Technicians.

If you were to compare ACCA and ICAEW to doing a degree and maybe CTA to a masters, AAT and ATT are like doing 'A' levels.

This is not to say that members cannot prepare accounts for you just as well – they may have as much practical experience as anyone else. Certainly, AAT would be a good qualification if you were looking for a bookkeeper to put your individual invoices into an accounting package or spreadsheet, ready for accounts to be produced.

103

Appendix 2 – Penalties for late filing and payment:

If you have a reasonable excuse for filing a tax return late, you may be able to appeal to HMRC to cancel penalties. There is no statutory definition of 'reasonable excuse', but HMRC gives some examples on their website:
- Death of a partner or close relative
- Unexpected stay in hospital
- A serious or live threatening illness
- Computer failures
- Service issues with HMRC's website
- A fire which prevented completion of a tax return
- Postal delays
- Delays relating to a disability you have.

If you missed the paper deadline, you can still submit a tax return online, but you will get a late filing penalty if you file a paper return late, even though it is within the deadline for filing online.

Late filing penalties (for self assessment):

If you file your tax return late you will be charged £100, regardless of whether you owe any tax.
If your tax return is over 3 months late, a daily penalty of up to £10, up to an overall total of £900 after 90 days can be applied.
If your tax return is over six months late, an additional £300 or 5% of the tax if greater can be charged.
If your tax return is over twelve months late, a further £300 or 5% of the tax due, again whichever is greater, can be charged.

Late payment:

As a self-assessment taxpayer, you will have to pay a balancing payment in the January following the end of the tax year, which takes into account the tax still to be paid, plus class 4 and class 2 National Insurance liabilities. You will also have to pay payments on account of next year's liability in January and July. These are equal to the tax that was due this year, with half payable in January and half in July.

If tax is paid late there are penalties:
30 days late – 5% of the tax due
6 months late – 5% of tax outstanding at that date
12 months – 5% of tax outstanding at that date

Interest can be also charged on unpaid tax or penalties. This is levied at the official rate of interest. At the time of writing the current rate was 2.00% and can be found on the HMRC website.

Appendix 3 - Partnership Tax Return – Form SA800:

I will not be covering this in a lot of detail as you will find that it follows the same conventions as the self-assessment tax return for an individual.

The main difference comes on page 6, where total profits from the partnership are summarised and you show there how those profits are attributed to the individual partners.
Profits will normally be shared according to the profit share percentage agreed by the partners in the partnership agreement. Often this will be an equal split, but sometimes one partner will have a greater share or will receive a small salary before the rest is divided up.
You then take what has been entered here to complete the partnership statement section of your personal tax return. That is to say that the partnership return reflects the total income and expenses of the whole partnership, including a section showing the share of the profits attributable to you; that share is then entered in the partnership section on the personal tax return.

Page 2: This page shows a series of six questions about the type of income received by the partnership.

There is also a description of the partnership's business and spaces to enter the accounting period of the partnership and the dates within the tax year that it has been trading.

Pages 3-5 are similar to equivalent pages in the self-employment section of the personal tax return.

Page 3: Concerns capital allowances claimed by the partnership.

Page 4: Is where you enter the profit & loss information for the partnership. See my notes on the self-employment pages of the personal tax return.

Page 5: Is for the partnership balance sheet.

Pages 6-7: A summary of the partnership profits is entered on **page 6** and then you show how the partnership profits are divided between the partners on the remainder of the page, on **page 7** and on any further duplicate pages.

These pages are then used to complete the partnership section of the personal tax return.

Page 8: The partnership return finishes with contact details and other information.

Appendix 4 -Making Tax Digital:

This is a new government initiative which aims to transform the tax system and bring about the end of the annual tax return.

It is not currently known what the fine details of the programme will be, but it seems likely the annual tax return will be replaced with a system of quarterly returns for self-employed people and companies. The plan was that other tax information such as bank interest would be fed straight into the individual's tax account removing the need for them to file a tax return.

In preparation for this the government has created personal tax accounts, which are available on request for any taxpayer. Presently you can login to them to see what tax you have paid in the year and any tax codes that have been applied to your income.

Since 1 April 2019 VAT registered businesses are required to keep digital records and use software to submit their VAT returns. Under this system, paper records no longer meet legal requirements set out in tax legislation. A business can continue to keep physical invoices & receipts, but each individual transaction will need to be recorded and stored digitally. Where records are maintained in more than one program there must be digital links between the software products or spreadsheets. 'Cut and paste' will not count as a digital link for these purposes, although it will be permissible to email a spreadsheet or put a digital record on a flashdrive for purposes of passing the records to an accountant or tax adviser. Records will have to contain certain basic information about the business and for individual transactions certain details such as the time of the supply and the rate of VAT applied.

In the future the government plans to expand this to collect more information and to replace the current system of personal and corporation tax returns.

Since 6 April 22 it is mandatory for all VAT registered businesses to submit their VAT returns using the Making Tax Digital system. That includes businesses below the VAT threshold, which were exempt until that point.

The introduction of additional measures for Making Tax Digital have recently been delayed. Under the current plans, self employed landlords will have to report their income and expenses on a quarterly basis from April 2026, but only if their income exceeds £50,000. From April 2027 the income threshold will be reduced to £30,000.

The ultimate plan is for partnerships and limited companies to also report under Making Tax Digital, but new dates for this have not yet been announced.

Appendix 5 – Preparing a simple set of accounts:

This chapter is to help you if you are self-employed and wanting to put together some accounts to include in your tax return.

There are two bases under which these can be prepared. The first is the cash basis, which means recording things as the money is paid out of your bank account and as money from sales is received.

The second is the accruals basis. The difference here is that sales are recorded on the date they are made, with your accounts showing a trade debtors balance for those sales which you have made but not yet been paid for. Similarly, purchases are recorded when the product or service is taken by the customer, rather than when they are actually paid for.

An example illustrating the difference between the two would be if you went to a DIY wholesale store and put some purchases on your account with the store. Under the cash basis you would only record the purchase when you cleared your tab, under the accruals basis you would record them when they were put on your tab.

You are allowed to report your turnover from trading on a cash basis if you are an unincorporated business and your turnover does not exceed £150,000.

To prepare a simple set of accounts (I will assume you are using the accruals basis for descriptive purposes), begin by listing out the following as they are at your accounting year end, which will most commonly be 5 April for an unincorporated business:
- (a) Fixed assets of the business – larger value items like a computer or expensive tools. Record these at the price you bought them for.
- (b) Bank balances and total cash held.
- (c) Value of any stock at the price you paid for it.
- (d) Trade debtors – any sales for which you have not yet been paid.
- (e) Trade creditors – any expenses of your business which you have been billed for, but not yet paid.
- (f) Bank loans taken out by the business.
- (g) Total sales made in the year.

(h) Total expenses suffered in the year – usually you would group these into different categories, such as: purchases, telephone, stationery, repairs, employee wages.

The second step is to convert these into a trial balance. Here you list the totals of each debtor, creditor, income and expense in a table. In the list above items a-d & h are shown as debits, items e-g as credits. The total debits and total credits should add up to the same number. If this is not your first year of trading, there will be a balancing figure which will be the profit retained from previous years.

This trial balance can then be turned into a set of accounts, the most simple form of which would be a two page document showing a profit and loss account on one page and a balance sheet on the other.

The profit and loss account is made up of the sales minus the expenses to give a profit for the year.

The balance sheet is made up of the fixed assets, stock, debtors, cash and bank, and creditors. There will be a balancing figure made up of the profit brought forward from previous years plus the profit for this year.

Appendix 6 – Tax mitigation for directors of small companies:

Until the removal of the dividend tax credit a few years ago the strategy that was best for extracting profits from a limited company with director shareholder/s was to pay a small salary accompanied with dividends up to their basic rate band.

However, since the dividend tax credit was removed, the situation has become slightly more complicated.

For the 2022/23 tax year you can pay a salary of £758 per month without paying tax or national insurance. To do this you must have registered as an employer and have made payroll returns to HMRC. You might consider as an alternative paying yourself a salary of up to £1,047 per month; in that case you would have to pay employer's national insurance, but not employee's national insurance.

If the directors are the only employees, you can avoid setting up a payroll scheme by paying yourself not more than £533 per month. However, you need to pay at least this amount and report it using a payroll scheme in order to get credit toward the state pension.

The above assumes that you don't have any other PAYE income, of course.

Assuming you do not have any other shares, you can pay dividends of up to £2,000 tax free. After that dividends will be taxed at 8.75% until you reach the higher rate threshold (for 22/23 total income of greater than £50,270).

(The dividend allowance will be reduced to £1,000 for 23/24 and then again to £500 for the 24/25 tax year).

The personal income tax allowance for 22/23 is £12,570, so if your total income is under that, you won't pay any income tax (although see above for the limits above which you would pay national insurance on a salary).

In addition, a company can provide an employee with one mobile phone tax free. The contract has to be between your company and the telecoms supplier.

There is also an exemption for trivial benefits. These are gifts to employees of up to £50. They cannot be cash or vouchers exchangeable for cash and for directors there is a limit of £300 per year.

This does mean, however, that your company could gift you a £50 voucher six times a year, as long as it is not exchangeable for cash.

114

References:

All the tax return pages shown in this book are © Crown copyright.

116

Thanks for reading

If you liked this book or found it useful, please leave a review.
Reviews help other readers find books.

If you are interested in reading some of my other books you can find details on:

My Amazon author page:
http://www.amazon.co.uk/H.-M.-Reynolds/e/B00JYJ5QXY/

My author page on Goodreads:
https://www.goodreads.com/author/show/8186896.H_M_Reynolds

My Facebook page:
https://www.facebook.com/AuthorHMReynolds/

Non Fiction by H M Reynolds

Japan Travelogue – my story and practical hints for planning a short holiday in Japan

A guide to the logistics of travelling between Kyoto and Tokyo and in the Kiso valley, particularly for first timers in Japan or those new to that region.

Fiction by H M Reynolds:

Emergency Protocol Nine

A collection of Science Fiction, Fantasy and Horror short stories.

ECOCIDE – an ecological sci-fi thriller

In the far future a revolutionary new space station has been created, a living creature built from biotechnology.

The technology is new,
the station is on the frontier of known space

and its commander is cracking under the pressure.
What could go wrong?

Harrin Meadows and a team of scientists are coming to the station - they will soon find out.